A MESSIANIC COMMENTARY

PAUL'S LETTER
TO

TITUS

HIS EMISSARY TO CRETE,
ABOUT CONGREGATIONAL LIFE

A MESSIANIC COMMENTARY

PAUL'S LETTER
TO

TITUS

HIS EMISSARY TO CRETE,
ABOUT CONGREGATIONAL LIFE

RABBI YOSEF KOELNER

Lederer Books
An imprint of
Messianic Jewish Publishers
Clarksville, MD 21029

Printed in the United States of America

Cover Design by Lisa Rubin, Messianic Jewish Publishers
Graphic Design by Yvonne Vermillion, MagicGraphix.com
Copy Editing by George Koch, copyedit.pro

2022   1

ISBN: 978-1-951833-24-4

Published by
Lederer Books
A division of
Messianic Jewish Publishers
6120 Day Long Lane
Clarksville, Maryland 21029

Distributed by
Messianic Jewish Resources Int'l.
www.MessianicJewish.net
Individual and Trade Order Line: 800-410-7647
Email: lederer@messianicjewish.net

DEDICATION

דּוֹר לְדוֹר, יְשַׁבַּח מַעֲשֶׂיךָ; וּגְבוּרֹתֶיךָ יַגִּידוּ.

Each generation will praise your works to the next
And proclaim your mighty acts.

Psalm 145:4

This commentary is dedicated to my father Isadore David Koelner ז״ל, who
instilled in me a love for the *Torah* and the Hebrew language.

ACKNOWLEDGMENTS

חַיִל מִי יִמְצָא-אֵשֶׁת?

[10] Who can find a capable wife?
Her value is far beyond that of pearls.
ב [11] Her husband trusts her from his heart,
And she will prove a great asset to him.
ג [12] She works to bring him good, not harm,
all the days of her life.

Proverbs 31:10–12

This commentary could not have been written
without the assistance of my dear wife Marty.
Since 1972 she has kindly and patiently
been editing my papers and manuscripts.

General Editor's Preface

Nearly all Bible commentators emphasize the importance of understanding the historical, cultural and grammatical aspects of any text of Scripture. As has been said, "A text without a context is a pretext." In other words, to assume one can understand what God has revealed through those who present his Word—prophets, poets, visionaries, apostles—without knowing the context is presumption. To really understand God's Word, it's essential to know something about who wrote it and to whom, what was actually said and what it originally meant, and when, where, and why it was written.

By now, everyone knows the New Testament is a thoroughly Jewish book, written entirely by Jews, taking place in and around Israel. The people written about—Paul, Peter, James, John, etc.—were all Jews who never abandoned their identities or people. The topics covered—sin, salvation, resurrection, Torah, Sabbath, how to "walk with God," the Millennium, etc.—were all Jewish topics that came from the Hebrew Scripture. Many expressions were Jewish idioms of that day. So, to fully understand the New Testament, it must be viewed through "Jewish eyes."

There are commentaries for women, men, teens, even children. There are commentaries that focus on financial issues in the Bible. Others provide archaeological material. Some commentaries are topical. Others are the works of eminent men and women of God. But until now, no commentary series has closely looked at the Jewish context of each of the New Testament books.

Some of the world's top Messianic Jewish theologians contributed their knowledge and understanding to this series. Each has written on a book or books of the New Testament they've specialized in, making sure to present the Jewish aspects—the original context—of each book. These works are not meant to be a verse-by-verse exegetical commentary. There are already many excellent ones available. But these commentaries supplement what others lack by focusing on the Jewish aspects along with explaining the book itself.

Several different authors wrote these commentaries, each in his own style. Just as the Gospels were written by four different men, each with his own perspective and style, these volumes too have variations. We didn't want the writers to have to conform too much to any particular style guide, other than our basic one.

You may see some Hebrew expressions or transliterations of Hebrew names in the New Testament. Thus, one writer might refer to the Apostle to the Gentiles as Paul. Another might write *Sha'ul*, Paul's Hebrew name. Still another might write *Saul*, an Anglicized version of *Sha'ul*. And some might write *Saul/Paul* to reflect, not reject, the different ways this servant of Messiah was known. Some offer both.

Another variation is the amount of reference material. Some have ample footnotes or endnotes, while others incorporate references within the text. Some don't have an enormous number of notes.

So, I invite you to put on your Jewish glasses and take a look at the New Testament in a way that will open up new understanding for you, as you get to know the God of Israel and his Messiah better.

RABBI BARRY RUBIN
General Editor and Publisher

THIS BOOK IS DIVIDED INTO FIVE MAIN SECTIONS:

- **Introduction: The Challenge Titus Faced** prepares readers for the content of Titus by explaining the historical context.

- **Outline of the Letter to Titus** simply gives a linear outline of the text of Titus, showing what topics are covered and where, which sets the stage for the text.

- **Text of the Letter to Titus** The text of the three chapters of Titus, from the *Complete Jewish Bible* (CJB) translation.

- **Verse-by-Verse Commentary**, which examines Titus' three chapters, providing an annotated discussion and analysis of each verse.

- **Ruminations and Illuminations** further expands on some of the various topics discussed and offers short analytical essays that are relevant to Titus and the various historical and religious contexts that surround it.

CONTENTS

I

INTRODUCTION
THE CHALLENGE TITUS FACED

THE TRIALS OF CONGREGATIONAL LIFE

The congregational issues addressed in the Letter to Titus transcend culture and are common to congregations in any state of development. Every congregation faces the challenges of organizing or reorganizing their structure, which includes policies and procedures. The appointing of qualified leaders as well as changes in leadership is ongoing. Leaders range from the rabbi/pastor to volunteers who participate in the worship team, teachers for the children, food programs, providing for the needy, missions programs, and every other conceivable ministry. All congregations sometimes face internal divisions, whether cultural, theological, or personal.

The Letter to Titus also emphasizes the importance of sound doctrine that is to be modeled and taught by Titus and his leadership team. It is important to understand that Crete had a significant and active Jewish population.[1] Paula Fredriksen, among others, informs us that throughout the Diaspora, it was common for non-Jews to regularly attend synagogue whether they were converts or not.[2] Consequently, the influential Circumcision Faction who were primarily non-Jewish former synagogue attenders brought unscriptural ideas such as "Jewish Myths" into the Messianic community (Titus 1:10–14). The introduction of these ideas created a rift in the community that Sha'ul instructed Titus to try to resolve. (Titus 1:5).

---

1. Refer to the section titled "The History of the Jewish People of Crete."
2. Paula Fredriksen, "If It Looks Like a Duck, and It Quacks Like a Duck…: On NOT Giving Up the 'God-Fearers,'" quoted in *Most Reliable Witness: Essays in Honor of Ross Shepard Kraemer*, 23–25.

1

There are at least ten major methods of interpreting the Pauline corpus. Six of these are discussed in this commentary. Maneuvering through these various streams of Pauline scholarship is an adventure. For me, it has been like cutting a path through a jungle, making fascinating discoveries along the way. Enjoy the adventure!

THE VAGARIES OF INTERPRETATION

The Pastoral Epistles

Titus as well as 1 and 2 Timothy are included in Sha'ul's group of letters known as the "Pastoral Epistles"—"pastoral" because they contain practical instructions for daily conduct, which was a type of *halakhah* for believers. "The root of the Hebrew term used to refer to Jewish law is *halakhah*, which means 'go' or 'walk.' *Halakhah*, then, is the 'way' a Jew is directed to behave in every aspect of life, encompassing civil, criminal and religious law."[3]

Based on the roles and functions of the men addressed, Dillon T. Thornton, in his work *Hostility in the House of God: An Investigation of the Opponents in 1 and 2 Timothy*, brushes aside the traditional designation of the "Pastoral Epistles" in favor of the designation "Letters to Paul's Delegates."[4] Both points of view have their merits.

The Challenge of Pauline Studies

The difficulty in writing a commentary on Titus is that there are a myriad of interpretative methods that leads to different conclusions regarding the meaning of Paul's writings. N. T. Wright compares Pauline Studies to "finding different ways up a mountain."[5] He discusses major categories of "schools" of Pauline interpretation. He describes these "schools" as "fighting over Paul's legacy," with each pushing a personal cultural agenda.[6] Each group has a specific focus,

---

3. "Halakhah: The Laws of Jewish Life." www.MyJewishLearning.com/article/halakhah-the-laws-of-jewish-life.
4. Dillon T. Thornton, *Hostility in the House of God: An Investigation of the Opponents in 1 and 2 Timothy*.
5. N. T. Wright, *Paul: In Fresh Perspective*, 2.
6. Wright, *Paul*, 13–16.

the major categories being historical, hermeneutical, cultural, and theological.[7] Joseph R. Dodson also denotes the variety of ways that scholars interpret Paul:

> Consider the remarks of Adolf von Harnack: "One might write a history of dogma as a history of the Pauline reactions in the church, and in doing so would touch on all the turning points of the history," and Wayne Meeks and John Fitzgerald: "[The] history of the reception of Paul's letters and of his story impresses upon us both the malleability of their meaning and the unending variety of ways that readers have injected their own identities into the process of interpretation."[8]

Furthermore, Daniel Boyarin compares Pauline Studies to a wrestling match. Quoting Maimonides, he goes on to say, "You will surely not find it strange that this subject, so profound and difficult, should bear various interpretations, for it will not impair the face of the argument with which we are here concerned. Either explanation may be adopted."[9]

The major Schools of Pauline Interpretation include:

1. The Historical Paul (HP): "Historians have been involved in what has been called the 'Quest for the Historical Jesus' for the past one hundred and seventy-five years, evaluating and sifting through our sources, trying to determine what we can reliably say about him. As it happens, the quest for the historical Paul began almost simultaneously, inaugurated by the German scholar Ferdinand Christian Baur."[10]

2. The Historical Epistolary Paul (HEP): Recognizes him as the undisputed author of only seven of his letters.[11]

3. The Paul of Acts (PACTS): Paula Fredriksen states, "In considering this very problem, I began by invoking Munck's rule of thumb: Acts can be relied upon where not contradicted by Paul.

---

7. Wright also discusses the issues of Pauline scholarship in his book *Paul and His Recent Interpreters*.

8. Michael F. Bird and Joseph R. Dodson, *Paul and the Second Century*, 13.

9. Daniel Boyarin, *A Radical Jew: Paul and the Politics of Identity*, 3.

10. James Tabor, "The Quest for the Historical Paul." www.BiblicalArchaeology.org/daily/people-cultures-in-the-bible/people-in-the-bible/the-quest-for-the-historical-paul.

11. Galatians, 1 Corinthians, 2 Corinthians, Romans, Philemon, Philippians and 1 Thessalonians.

But I was more cautious: Acts, I think, can be used (a) where corroborated by Paul; and (b) where corroborated by what we can know from other sources, especially inscriptions.[12]

4. New Perspective on Paul (NPP): This movement's founder, E. P. Sanders, introduced his ideas in *Paul and Palestinian Judaism*. N.T. Wright was the first to use the term "new perspective on Paul." The NPP claims first-century Judaism was not a merit-based religion, but a covenant community created by God's grace. Far from suffering the affliction of an introspective conscience, and a struggle to keep the law by works-righteousness, mainstream Judaism understood that through God's covenant they were already right with him. The Law (*nomos*) was not a means of getting saved but of staying saved. Keeping God's Law was the appropriate response to God's covenant mercy.[13] The NPP has developed many subsets.

5. Paul Within Judaism (PWJ): A subset that builds on NPP. According to Professor Steve Mason, PWJ finds the NPP and its ilk too encrusted with vestigial church language, in continuing to speak of pre-70 C.E. "Christianity," "Christians," "churches," "missionaries," "faith/belief," and the like. They call for a more radical perspective, which begins from the assumption—and ends with the conclusion—that Paul lived wholly "within Judaism." They want a new vocabulary that does not traffic in distinctively Christian language, which they see as anachronistic.[14] Especially pertinent are Jewish scholars who are not Yeshua followers who do not view Sha'ul as a de-Judaized Jew but as a practicing first-century Jew. Among this growing list of scholars are Pinchas Lapide, Hyam Maccoby, Alan Segal, Daniel Boyarin, Amy-Jill Levine, Marc Zvi Brettler, Mark Nanos, Pamela Eisenbaum and Paula Fredriksen.

---

12. Paula Fredriksen, "Putting Paul in His (Historical) Place," in *Journal of the Jesus Movement in Its Jewish Setting*, Issue 5. See also Irinia Levinskaya, *The Book of Acts in Its Diaspora Setting*.
13. Ligon Duncan, "N.T. Wright and the New Perspective on Paul."
    https://www.ligonier.org/learn/articles/nt-wright-and-new-perspective-paul.
14. Steve Mason, "Paul Without Judaism: Historical Method Over Perspective," in *Paul and Matthew Among Jews and Gentiles: Essays in Honor of Terence L. Donaldson*, 1.

6. Messianic Jewish Perspective (MJP): Mark S. Kinzer proposes: The emergence of the Messianic Jewish movement has profound hermeneutical implications. For the first time since the creation of the New Testament canon, a community exists which treats that canon as authoritative and also identifies itself with the Jewish people and its history. Messianic Jews require no imaginative leap to read these texts as Jewish writings. Instead, such a leap is demanded of us when asked to consider that the New Testament might have non- or anti-Jewish elements.[15]

This commentary employs the Messianic Jewish Perspective, which is largely supported by the NPP and its PWP subset.

A SUBTEXT WE MIGHT HAVE MISSED

While I was re-editing the manuscript for this commentary, it dawned on me that the Letter to Titus contained a not-so-apparent subtext. Sha'ul, as a father, was writing to his son, Titus, who was tired and somewhat discouraged. The following is my synopsis of what Sha'ul wrote.

Titus, my dear son —

Remain confident that what I have taught you is reliable and trustworthy because I have received it directly from Yeshua the Messiah. What Yeshua revealed to me is sound doctrine and needs to be proclaimed on the island of Crete because it leads to salvation and a godly life.

I need you to complete several arduous tasks before you complete your assignment in Crete.

I want to let you know that your replacements are on the way— Artemis, Tychius, Zenas, and Apollo. Once they arrive and are apprised of the situation, you can join me at Nicopolis.

With love and appreciation,

Abba Sha'ul

---

15. Mark Kinzer, "A Messianic Jewish Perspective on Luke-Acts."
   www.academia.edu/es/42027810/A_Messianic_Jewish_Perspective_on_Luke_Acts.

TWINS DIVIDED IN THE WOMB

In *Judaism in the Beginning of Christianity*, Jacob Neusner asserts, "The history of 'Christianity' begins in Israel, the Jewish people, and in Judaism."[16] Daniel Boyarin states, "For at least the first three centuries of their common lives, Judaism in all of its forms and Christianity in all of its forms were part of one complex religious family, twins in a womb, contending with each other for identity and precedence, but sharing with each other the same spiritual food."[17]

Eventually Christianity and Judaism developed their own individual identities and emerged as two separate faith traditions. The premise of Shaye J. D. Cohen's article "The Ways That Parted" is correct when he argues that the separation of Christianity from Judaism was a process, not an event.[18] The essential part of this process was that the church was becoming more and more Gentile and less and less Jewish, but the separation manifested itself in different ways in each local community where Jews and Yeshua followers dwelt together. In some places, the Jews expelled the followers of Yeshua; in other places, the believers left of their own accord.

According to the *Jewish Virtual Library*, "Whatever the nature of the relationship of Jesus to the various Jewish groups of his time [Pharisees, Sadducees, and others—including the Essenes and Qumran Covenanters], the New Testament reflects a stage of development when relations between Jews and Christians had already begun to deteriorate. Hence, the New Testament describes Jesus as engaged in violent polemics against the 'Scribes and Pharisees,' and especially against the interpretation of *Torah* and Judaism which they represented."[19]

---

16. Jacob Neusner, *Judaism in the Beginning of Christianity*, 9–10.
17. Daniel Boyarin, "Dying for God: Martyrdom and the Making of Christianity and Judaism," *History of Religions* 42.2, 175–180.
18. Shaye J. D. Cohen, "The Ways That Parted: Jews, Christians, and Jewish Christians, ca. 100–150 C.E.", in *Jews and Christians in the First and Second Centuries: The Interbellum 70–132 C.E.*, 307–339.
19. "Religion: Christianity." https://www.JewishVirtualLibrary.org/christianity-2.

Jerome D. Quinn and most commentators agree that the Messianic community in Crete was predominately Jewish.[20] However, the inclusion of non-Jews into the Messianic community, as well as Sha'ul's opposition to the strict application of Jewish customs for Gentile converts, exacerbated the growing theological divide between the "twins in the womb."[21]

Lawrence H. Schiffman emphasizes the Jewish community's difficulty with the inclusion of non-Jews into the Messianic community: "The Tania gradually found themselves facing a 'messianic' movement whose members were not Jews from the point of view of *halakhah* [Jewish law]. To the rabbis, they were not Jews with incorrect views about the messiah but gentiles who claimed to be the true Israel."[22] Andreas J. Köstenberger further attests that in Crete similar issues existed between believers of Jewish and Gentile descent.[23]

Both the Letter to Titus and various extra-biblical literature illustrate and record the development of the schism between the "twins in the womb."

THE HISTORY OF THE JEWISH PEOPLE OF CRETE

In Titus' time, Crete was a Roman province. The Roman proconsul, or governor, ruled the province from Gortyna, the most prosperous city in Crete during Hellenistic times. Jewish communities on Crete are first mentioned in 4th-century-B.C.E. epitaphs from Kassanoi and Kissamos. In Kissamos, a "Sophia of Gortyna, an elder and leader of the synagogue," is mentioned and attests to the leading role of women in Diaspora communities.[24]

---

20. Jerome D. Quinn, *The Anchor Bible: A New Translation with Notes and Commentary and an Introduction to Titus, I and II Timothy, The Pastoral Epistles,* 16.
21. Sha'ul's opposition is clearly demonstrated in the Book of Galatians.
22. Lawrence Schiffman. https://www.MyJewishLearning.com/article/how-jewish-christians-became-christians.
23. Andreas Köstenberger, T. Desmond Alexander, and Thomas Schreiner, *Commentary on 1–2 Timothy and Titus,* 188.
24. "The History of the Jews of Crete." www.Etz-Hayyim-Hania.org/the-jews-of-crete/the-history-of-the-jews-of-crete.

The earliest evidence of a Jewish community in Crete is in a circular letter from the Roman Senate (142 B.C.E.), in support of the Jews, written to various countries at the request of Simeon the Hasmonean. This letter was also forwarded to Gortyna (I Macc. 15:15–24). The author of the *Sibylline Oracles* attests that by 140 B.C.E. the entire land [Crete] and sea was "full of Jews."[25]

> By the time of the Roman conquest of Crete in the 1st century B.C.E., Jewish communities were thriving in most of the major cities including Gortyna, Kissamos, Hania, Rethymnon, Knossos and Sitia. In the 1st century C.E., Roman historian Tacitus provides an intriguing theory regarding the origin of Jews. He claims that the Jews were, in fact, Cretans and that their original name was "Idaeans" (in other words, "from Mt. Ida"). Beyond the obvious etymological similarity, his theory may also be based on part of the tradition linking the Philistines to the Eteo-Cretans who were fleeing the island following the arrival of the so-called Sea Peoples ca. 1200 B.C.E.[26]

In 40 C.E., the Hellenistic Jewish philosopher Philo wrote in *Legatio ad Gaium* that the mainlands were full of Jewish colonies, as was Crete, the most highly esteemed of the islands. Gortyna was the center of Jewish life on Crete and is strategically located on its southern coast. After the Romans conquered Crete, in 67 B.C.E., Gortyna became the Roman provincial capital. The province also included Cyrene in North Africa, in present-day Libya. Subsequently, Gortyna rose to prominence, attracting Jewish artisans and technicians from Alexandria. Scholars agree that the Jewish community of Crete had its primary origins there.[27]

---

25. Stylianos Spyridakis, "Notes on the Jews of Gortyna and Crete," in *Zeitschrift für Papyrologie und Epigraphik* 73.
26. "History of the Jews of Crete."
27. Jirair Tashjian, "Life in Crete at the Time of Titus." https://SundayTeacher.com/vcmedia/2414/2414925.pdf.

The Origin of the Messianic Jewish Community of Crete

The prevailing hypothesis is that the origin of the Messianic Jewish community of Crete coincides with a visit from Rav Sha'ul (Paul) to Crete, where he proclaimed the Good News to its inhabitants. The Orthodox Church of Crete subscribes to this hypothesis and states: "The first Christian nucleus was formed here around 64 C.E. by St. Paul, during his 4th missionary journey. Paul assigned to his disciple Titus, who became the first Bishop of Crete, the systematic teaching of Christianity on the island."[28] Robert Logan and Neil Cole reflect this prevailing sentiment: "Apparently Paul introduced Christianity in Crete when he and Titus visited the island, after which he left Titus there to organize the converts."[29] If Sha'ul did evangelize Crete, when he did is unknown, as his visit to Crete is not recorded as part of his missionary journeys in Acts.

However, based on the internal evidence in the Book of Acts, I contend that it is reasonable to conclude that the Messianic community of Crete had its origins on the day of *Shavuot* (Pentecost). Howard Marshall, in his article "The Significance of Pentecost," has a similar view:

> The immediate Lucan context for the events of Pentecost is provided by the words of the risen Jesus to the disciples. Luke has divided the account of this conversation into two parts, one of which provides the conclusion to the Gospel, which thus ends on a forward-looking note, and the other at the beginning of Acts, which correspondingly commences with a clear link with the past. So in Luke 24:49 after the disciples have been commanded to preach repentance and forgiveness to all the nations, and have been appointed witnesses, they are told, "Behold, I send the promise of my Father upon you; but stay in the city, until you are clothed with power from on high." There is a similar statement in Acts 1:4, where we are told that Jesus commanded the disciples not to depart from Jerusalem, "but to wait

---

28. "The Church of Crete." http://OrthodoxCrete.com/en/the-church-of-crete,
29. Robert E. Logan and Neil Cole, *Beyond Church Planting*.

for the promise of the Father." At this point Luke makes Jesus break into direct speech—"The promise of the Father, which," he said, "you heard from me, for John baptized with water but before many days you shall be baptized with the Holy Spirit." (Acts 1:8) [30]

The Promise of the Father, the *Ruach HaKodesh* (Holy Spirit), was first received by the twelve Apostles and the 120 on *Shavuot*. They formed the group that had been waiting in obedience to Yeshua's command to remain in Jerusalem in anticipation of the Father's promise. [31]

> [1] The festival of *Shavu'ot* arrived, and the believers all gathered together in one place. [2] Suddenly there came a sound from the sky like the roar of a violent wind, and it filled the whole house where they were sitting. [3] Then they saw what looked like tongues of fire, which separated and came to rest on each one of them. [4] They were all filled with the *Ruach HaKodesh* and began to talk in different languages, as the Spirit enabled them to speak. (Acts 2:1–4)

This event immediately drew a crowd—a crowd of Jews who had come to Jerusalem from all over the world—including Crete—to observe the festival.

> [5] Now there were staying in Yerushalayim religious Jews from every nation under heaven. [6] When they heard this sound, a crowd gathered; they were confused, because each one heard the believers speaking in his own language. [7] Totally amazed, they asked, "How is this possible? Aren't all these people who are speaking from the Galil? [8] How is it that we hear them speaking in our native languages? [9] We are Parthians, Medes, Elamites; residents of Mesopotamia, Y'hudah, Cappadocia, Pontus, Asia, [10] Phrygia, Pamphylia, Egypt, the parts of Libya near Cyrene; visitors from Rome; [11] Jews by birth and proselytes; *Jews from Crete* [ital. added] and from Arabia!" How is it that we hear them speaking in our own languages about the great things God has done?" [12] Amazed and confused, they all went on asking each other, "What can this mean?"

30. Howard Marshall, "The Significance of
    Pentecost." https://place.asburyseminary.edu/asburyjournal/vol32/iss2/5.
31. Hilary Le Cornu and Joseph Shulam, *A Commentary on the Jewish Roots of Acts*, 37.

¹³ But others made fun of them and said, "They've just had too much wine!" (Acts 2:5–13)

Kefa (Peter) then addressed the crowd with a salvation message:

¹⁴ Then Kefa stood up with the Eleven and raised his voice to address them: "You Judeans, and all of you [including the Jews from Crete] staying here in Yerushalayim! Let me tell you what this means! Listen carefully to me! …

³⁶ Therefore, let the whole house of Isra'el know beyond doubt that God has made him both Lord and Messiah—this Yeshua, whom you executed on a stake!"

³⁷ On hearing this, they [including Jews from Crete] were stung in their hearts; and they said to Kefa and the other emissaries, "Brothers, what should we do?" ³⁸ Kefa answered them, "Turn from sin, return to God, and each of you be immersed on the authority of Yeshua the Messiah into forgiveness of your sins, and you will receive the gift of the *Ruach HaKodesh*! ³⁹ For the promise is for you, for your children, and for those far away—as many as *ADONAI* our God may call!" ⁴⁰ He pressed his case with many other arguments and kept pleading with them, "Save yourselves from this perverse generation!" ⁴¹ So those who accepted what he said were immersed, and there were added to the group that day about three thousand people. (Acts 2:1–14, 36–41)

The 3000 who responded to Kefa's message received the gift of the *Ruach HaKodesh*, which empowered them to share the Good News about Yeshua HaMashiach. It is not unreasonable to conclude that among the 3000 who were saved were Jews from the Diaspora, *including Jews from Crete* [ital. added], who would then return to their respective homelands at the conclusion of *Shavuot*, setting in motion the beginning of the fulfillment of the Great Commission.[32]

It is interesting to note that the Orthodox Church in America accepts the tradition that Titus was present at *Shavuot*.

---

32. For a closer study of the rituals associated with Shavuot, see "Power From on High – *Shavuot*, Sivan 6, 30 C.E."

> At Jerusalem, Saint Titus saw the Lord. He heard His preaching and believed in Him. He witnessed the suffering and death of the Savior on the Cross, His glorious Resurrection and Ascension to Heaven. On the day of Pentecost the future apostle heard how the Twelve Apostles, after the descent of the Holy Spirit, spoke in various languages, among which was the Cretan language. (Acts 2:11) [33]

It is my opinion, therefore, that Sha'ul and Titus did indeed visit Crete, but that there was already a fledgling community of believers there whose origin can be traced back to *Shavuot*. Their visit, and Sha'ul's subsequent charge to Titus, was to help organize and strengthen the existing Messianic community.

---

33. "Apostle Titus of the Seventy and Bishop of Crete."
   https://www.OCA.org/saints/lives/2018/08/25/102393-apostle-titus-of-the-seventy-and-bishop-of-crete.

2

OUTLINE OF THE LETTER TO TITUS

I. Titus 1:1–4		The Salutation of the Writer Sha'ul the Shaliach (Apostle)
	A. 1:1a	Sha'ul establishes his authority as a *shaliach*
	B. 1:1b	Sha'ul emphasizes the purpose of his calling
	C. 1:2–3	Sha'ul affirms the certainty of the Gospel
	D. 1:4a	Sha'ul defines his relationship with Titus
	E. 1:4b	Sha'ul blesses God's elect in Crete
II. Titus 1:5–16		Sha'ul's Instructions to His Designated Emissary Titus
	A. 1:5	Establishing order among God's Chosen People
	B. 1:5b–9	Appointing leaders and qualifications for *zeqenim* (elders)
	C. 1:10–14	Addressing community controversies caused by false teachers
	D. 1:15–16	Clarifying Jewish purity laws
III. Titus 2:1–15		Instructions for Various Groups of Believers
	A. 2:1	The importance of sound doctrine
	B. 2:2–11	Various groups
	i. 2:2–3	Older men and older women
	ii. 2:5	Younger women
	iii. 2:6	Younger men
	iv. 2:7	Titus should exemplify godly behavior
	v. 2:9–10	Slaves

3

TEXT OF THE LETTER TO TITUS

TITUS 1

[1] From: Sha'ul, God's slave and an emissary of Yeshua the Messiah, sent to promote among God's chosen people the trust and knowledge of truth which led to godliness [2] and which are based on the certain hope of eternal life. God, who does not lie, promised that life before the beginning of time [3] but made public this word of his in its own season through a proclamation with which I have been entrusted by order of God, our Deliverer.

[4] To: Titus, a true son in the faith we share:

> Grace and *shalom* from God the Father and from the Messiah Yeshua, our Deliverer.

[5] The reason I left you in Crete was so that you might attend to the matters still not in order and appoint congregation leaders in each city—those were my instructions. [6] A leader must be blameless, husband to one wife, with believing children who do not have a reputation for being wild or rebellious. [7] For an overseer, as someone entrusted with God's affairs, must be blameless—he must not be self-willed or quick-tempered, he must not drink excessively, get into fights or be greedy for dishonest gain. [8] On the contrary, he must be hospitable, devoted to good, sober-mindedness, uprightness, holiness and self-control. [9] He must hold firmly to the trustworthy Message that agrees with the doctrine; so that by his sound teaching he will be able to exhort and encourage, and also to refute those who speak against it.

[10] For there are many, especially from the Circumcision faction, who are rebellious, who delude people's minds with their worthless and

misleading talk. [11] They must be silenced; because they are upsetting entire households by teaching what they have no business teaching and doing it for the sake of dishonest gain. [12] Even one of the Cretans' own prophets has said, "Cretans are always liars, evil brutes, lazy gluttons"—[13] and it's true! For this reason, you must be severe when you rebuke those who have followed this false teaching, so that they will come to be sound in their trust [14] and no longer pay attention to Judaistic myths or to the commands of people who reject the truth.

[15] To all who are themselves pure, everything is pure. But to those who are defiled and without trust, nothing is pure—even their minds and consciences have been defiled. [16] They claim to know God, but with their actions they deny him. They are detestable and disobedient; they have proved themselves unfit to do anything good.

TITUS 2

[1] But you, explain what kind of behavior goes along with sound teaching. [2] Tell the older men to be serious, sensible, self-controlled and sound in their trust, love and perseverance.

[3] Likewise, tell the older women to behave the way people leading a holy life should. They shouldn't be slanderers or slaves to excessive drinking. They should teach what is good, [4] thus training the younger women to love their husbands and children, [5] to be self-controlled and pure, to take good care of their homes and submit to their husbands. In this way, God's message will not be brought into disgrace.

[6] Similarly, urge the young men to be self-controlled, [7] and in everything set them an example yourself by doing what is good. When you are teaching, have integrity and be serious; [8] let everything you say be so wholesome that an opponent will be put to shame because he will have nothing bad to say about us.

[9] Tell slaves to submit to their masters in everything, to give satisfaction without talking back [10] or pilfering. On the contrary, they

should demonstrate complete faithfulness always, so that in every way they will make the teaching about God our Deliverer more attractive.

[11] For God's grace, which brings deliverance, has appeared to all people. [12] It teaches us to renounce godlessness and worldly pleasures, and to live self-controlled, upright and godly lives now, in this age; [13] while continuing to expect the blessed fulfillment of our certain hope, which is the appearing of the *Sh'khinah* of our great God and the appearing of our Deliverer, Yeshua the Messiah. [14] He gave himself up on our behalf in order to free us from all violation of *Torah* and purify for himself a people who would be his own, eager to do good.

[15] These are the things you should say. Encourage and rebuke with full authority; don't let anyone look down on you.

TITUS 3

[1] Remind people to submit to the government and its officials, to obey them, to be ready to do any honorable kind of work, [2] to slander no one, to avoid quarrelling, to be friendly, and to behave gently towards everyone.

[3] For at one time, we too were foolish and disobedient, deceived and enslaved by a variety of passions and pleasures. We spent our lives in evil and envy; people hated us, and we hated each other. [4] But when the kindness and love for mankind of God our Deliverer was revealed, [5] he delivered us. It was not on the ground of any righteous deeds we had done, but on the ground of his own mercy. He did it by means of the *mikveh* of rebirth and the renewal brought about by the *Ruach HaKodesh,* [6] whom he poured out on us generously through Yeshua the Messiah, our Deliverer. [7] He did it so that by his grace we might come to be considered righteous by God and become heirs, with the certain hope of eternal life. [8] You can trust what I have just said, and I want you to speak with confidence about these things, so that those who have put their trust in God may apply themselves to doing good deeds. These are both good in themselves and valuable to the community.

⁹ But avoid stupid controversies, genealogies, quarrels and fights about the *Torah*; because they are worthless and futile. ¹⁰ Warn a divisive person once, then a second time; and after that, have nothing more to do with him. ¹¹ You may be sure that such a person has been perverted and is sinning: he stands self-condemned.

¹² When I send Artemas or Tychicus to you. Do your best to come to me in Nicopolis, for I have decided to spend the winter there. ¹³ Do your best to help Zenas the *Torah* expert and Apollos with their arrangements for travelling, so that they will lack nothing. ¹⁴ And have our people learn to apply themselves to doing good deeds that meet genuine needs, so that they will not be unproductive.

¹⁵ All who are with me send you greetings. Give our greetings to our friends in the faith.

Grace be with you all.

4

VERSE-BY-VERSE COMMENTARY

Fundamental to one's understanding of Sha'ul's theology is his background in Judaism, in particular his training as a Pharisee, which he filtered through his initial and subsequent revelations concerning the Messiahship of Yeshua of Nazeret.[1] N.T. Wright concurs:

> Paul's worldview is a thoroughly Jewish one (and it would have been recognized as such by Paul's contemporaries). Paul is a Pharisee who has "rethought and reworked every aspect of his native Jewish theology in light of the messiah and the spirit."[2]

The readjustment of his theology began on the road to Damascus:

> [3] He was on the road and nearing Dammesek, when suddenly a light from heaven flashed all around him. [4] Falling to the ground, he heard a voice saying to him, "Sha'ul! Sha'ul! Why do you keep persecuting me?" [5] "Sir, who are you?" he asked. "I am Yeshua, and you are persecuting me. [6] But get up, and go into the city, and you will be told what you have to do." (Acts 9:3–6)

Beyond God's personal revelation, Sha'ul's new mission was further explained to him by Hananyah (Ananias), a devout and respected leader in both the Messianic and traditional Jewish communities.

> [12] A man named Hananyah, an observant follower of the *Torah* who was highly regarded by the entire Jewish community there, [13] came to me, stood by me and said, "Brother Sha'ul, see again!" And at that

---

1. For a more in-depth study of the Sha'ul's training as a Pharisee, see the essays "Sha'ul the Pharisee" and "Foundational Principles of Rabbinic Judaism."
2. Wright, *Paul*, 185.

very moment, I recovered my sight and saw him. [14] He said, "The God of our fathers determined in advance that you should know his will, see the *Tzaddik* and hear his voice; [15] because you will be a witness for him to everyone[3] of what you have seen and heard. [16] So now, what are you waiting for? Get up, immerse yourself and have your sins washed away as you call on his name." (Acts 22:12–16)

After a few days, Sha'ul took his first steps to fulfilling his newfound calling ... "and immediately he began proclaiming in the synagogues that Yeshua is the Son of God" (Acts 22:20).

CHAPTER ONE

Verses 1–4

[1] From: Sha'ul, God's slave and an emissary of Yeshua the Messiah, sent to promote among God's chosen people the trust and knowledge of truth which led to godliness [2] and which are based on the certain hope of eternal life. God, who does not lie, promised that life before the beginning of time [3] but made public this word of his in its own season through a proclamation with which I have been entrusted by order of God, our Deliverer.

[4] To: Titus, a true son in the faith we share: Grace and *shalom* from God the Father and from the Messiah Yeshua, our Deliverer.

Verse 1

From: Sha'ul The writer of the Letter to Titus identifies himself as Sha'ul (Saul) of Tarsus, commonly known as the Apostle Paul. He has been the undisputed author of Titus since the second century. Some of the early advocates of Pauline authorship are Tertullian, Origen, and Clement of Alexandria,[4] as well as Eusebius of Caesarea.[5]

---

3. "Everyone" means "the *Goyim*, even to their kings, and to the sons of Isra'el as well" (cf. Acts 9:15).
4. Peter Kirby, "e-Catena: Compiled Allusions to the NT in the Ante-Nicene Fathers – Titus." www.EarlyChristianWritings.com/e-catena/titus1.html.
5. Philip Schaff, *History of the Christian Church, Volume III: Nicene and Post-Nicene Christianity. A.D. 311–600.*

Conservative scholars also support Pauline authorship. Donald Guthrie, in his book *The Pastoral Epistles*, gives an extensive list of conservative scholars who affirm Paul as the author.

Some modern scholars, though, attribute the pastoral letters to an anonymous author. Guthrie also includes the history of the development of the theory that Paul was *not* the author of these letters.[6] This commentary accepts the traditional view that Sha'ul of Tarsus was the author of Titus. It is believed to have been written just before the destruction of the Temple, circa 63 C.E.

God's slave [servant]. Initially, to establish his authority, Sha'ul frames his ministry as that of *eved Adonai*, "servant of Adonai." This phrase is a common expression in the *Tanakh*.

The Hebrew word *eved* (*doulos* in Greek) can be understood figuratively as "slave" and, in this sense, means "a person or persons who are devoted to the well-being of others in the service of God"[7] (Joel 2:29, Zech. 1:6, Jer. 7:25, Ez. 38:17, Amos 3:7). Examples where *doulos* is often translated as "slave" in the New Testament include Romans 1:1 and Philippians 1:1.

But "servant of the Lord" is also a title of honor often associated with specific individuals HaShem has chosen to lead his people. This phrase is used in the *Tanakh* for Abraham (Gen. 26:24), Moses (Jos. 1:1), and many other leaders such as the Patriarchs (Deut. 9:27; cf. Ps. 105:6, 42), Joshua (24:29; Judg. 2:8), David (Ps. 18, 36, captions), the Prophets (Jer. 7:25, 25:4, et al.), Isaiah (20:3), Job (1:8, 2:3, 42:7) and even Nebuchadnezzar (Jer. 25:9, 27:6, 43:10).[8]

Thus, by using the term *eved Adonai*, Sha'ul is saying that, just like Avraham, Moshe, Joshua, David and the prophets, he (Sha'ul) also is God's chosen servant-slave/servant-leader "who is devoted to the well-being of others in the service of God."

---

6. Donald Guthrie, *New Testament Introduction*: The Pauline Epistles, 23.

7. Amy-Jill Levine and Marc Zvi Brettler, *The Jewish Annotated New Testament: New Revised Standard Version Bible Translation*, 301.

8. Emil G. Hirsch, "Servant of God." https://www.jewishencyclopedia.com/articles/13444-servant-of-god.

An emissary [*shaliach*, "apostle"] **of Yeshua the Messiah:** Sha'ul further establishes his authority as an approved leader in the Messianic movement by declaring himself a *shaliach* of Yeshua HaMashiach. The phrase *shaliach* of Yeshua HaMashiach connects Sha'ul's role as a servant of Adonai with his ministry as an apostle commissioned by Yeshua (Acts 9:15; 1 Tim. 2:7; 2 Tim. 1:11). Hermann Vogelstein clearly states that the concept of the *shaliach* "must be understood from a historical point of view as having developed out of the Jewish apostolate."[9]

The Pharisees embraced the concept of being sent to a particular community as a *shaliach*.

> "Woe to you hypocritical *Torah*-teachers and *P'rushim*! You go about [as a *shaliach*] over land and sea to make one proselyte; and when you succeed, you make him twice as fit for Gei-Hinnom as you are!" (Mt. 23:15)

In its Jewish context, *shaliach* can be a person "who, whether a man or woman, was the agent or emissary of the sender: the concept of *shaliah shel' adam kemoto* ['a person's agent is as the person himself'] and thus fully representative of the sender.[10] Inherent in this definition is the idea of being chosen as a representative of a higher power such as God or a king and of having the authority to transmit the message of the one who sent him. Vogelstein says, "This office is found as early as at the time of the composition of the Books of Chronicles. Two categories of apostles could be ascertained, viz. (1) apostles of the central authorities to the various communities, and (2) apostles of the communities to the various central authorities."[11]

As Sha'ul had been commissioned by Yeshua (Acts 9:3–6) and his calling had been affirmed by the Apostles in Jerusalem (9:26–28), the Messianic community in Crete, predominantly from a Jewish background, would have been familiar with the office of a *shaliach*, enabling them to accept the full weight of Sha'ul's authority and message as given to him by Yeshua HaMashiach and affirmed by the Apostles.

---

9. Hermann Vogelstein, *The Development of the Apostolate in Judaism and Its Transformation in Christianity,* 100.
10. Levine and Brettler, *Jewish Annotated New Testament,* 112.
11. Vogelstein, *Development,* 99.

Sent: The word "sent/send" is to be understood in the same sense as *shaliachim*. Ezra is an example of the prototype *shaliach* as he was **sent** as the representative (*shaliach*) of King Artaxerxes to the Jewish community in Jerusalem (Ezra 7:14). In a similar fashion, Artaxeres **sends** Nehemiah to Jerusalem to authorize the rebuilding of the city of Jerusalem (Neh. 2:5).

In the *Brit Chadashah* (New Covenant), one of the clearest examples of the Jewish concept of an apostle can be found in the synoptic Gospels where Yeshua appoints or commissions his twelve *talmidim* (disciples) as *shaliachim* (apostles) (Mt. 10:1–2; cf. Mk. 3:13–19a; Lk. 6:12–16). According to Heinrich Schuetz, the phrase "sent out" as it appears in Mark is the literal translation of the Hebrew expression חילש השע, which in all cases has the significance of "to appoint as a plenipotentiary (an authorized representative)."[12]

God's chosen people: *B'Chirai Adonai* – God's Chosen or Elect. David Flusser suggests the phrase "God's chosen or elect" (*B'Chirai Adonai*) was a common self-definition used to describe the faith community of the first-century disciples of Yeshua.[13] This term has its roots in the *Tanakh*. In the *Torah*, the children of Israel are called God's chosen people (Deut. 7:6) and the designation is also found in the prophets and writings (Isa. 65:9; Ps. 105:43). In Isaiah 65:9, the phrase God's "chosen" links election to servanthood.[14]

> [9] I will bring forth descendants from Ya'akov,
> heirs of my mountains from Y'hudah;
> my **chosen** ones will possess them,
> and my **servants** will live there. (Isa. 65:9)

However, a key element of Rav Sha'ul's commission as a *shaliach* was to unfold the "mystery" of the message of Messiah Yeshua, which declares that, concerning the promises of God, the *nations* have become joint heirs with God's chosen people—*B'Chirai Adonai*.[15] Therefore, in the light of the seemingly radical revelation that "through the Good News the Gentiles were to be joint heirs, a joint body, and joint sharers with the Jews in what God has promised" (Eph. 2:19–3:6), Sha'ul refers to *all* the members of the Messianic community in Crete—Jews and non-Jews alike—as God's *B'chirai Adonai*.

---

12. Vogelstein, *Development*, 99.
13. David Flusser, *Judaism and the Origins of Christianity*, 30.
14. Levine and Brettler, *Jewish Annotated New Testament*, 398.
15. Eph. 2:19–3:6.

Today, common church doctrine teaches that through faith and discipleship, Yeshua's followers are the elect. Frank Gaebelein defines God's chosen as those who have responded to God's call through the Gospel.[16] The elect or chosen are those who have become true partakers of the Christian salvation—contrasted with those who have been invited to join God's household and participate in the work of his Kingdom but who have not shown themselves fitted to obtain it.[17]

Verses 2–3

Sent to promote ... the trust and knowledge of truth which lead to godliness [2] and which are based on the certain hope of eternal life. God ... [3] made public this word of his in its own season through a proclamation with which I have been entrusted by order of God, our Deliverer.

This reflects the underlying theme of the Letter to Titus: The message that Sha'ul has taught and transmitted to Titus is reliable and trustworthy because Sha'ul received it directly from Yeshua the Messiah. What Yeshua revealed to Sha'ul, in contrast to the erroneous message of the Circumcision Faction, is sound doctrine and needs to be proclaimed on the island of Crete because it leads to eternal salvation and a godly life.

God who does not lie, promised: God's promises are truthful and reliable. This phrase is a direct reference to Bil'am's prophecy concerning Israel, in Numbers 23:19-

> God is not a human who lies
> or a mortal who changes his mind.
> When he says something, he will do it;
> when he makes a promise, he will fulfill it.

In contrast, the Cretans who are the members of the Circumcision Faction are liars (Titus 1:12–13). Their doctrines are unsound as well as unreliable.

---

16 Frank E. Gaebelein, J. D. Douglas, and Dick Polcyn, *The Expositor's Bible Commentary, Volume 11*, 427.

17 Carl Ludwig Willibald Grimm, et al., *The New Thayer's Greek-English Lexicon of the New Testament*.

Verse 4

To: Titus The letter is addressed to Titus. His name, Titus (Greek: Τίτος), which is of unknown meaning, is possibly related to the Latin *titulus*, "title of honor." However, it is more likely of Oscan origin, since it was borne by the legendary Sabine king Titus Tatius.[18] Titus is mentioned fifteen times in four unique forms in the New Covenant and first appears in 2 Corinthians 2:13. Chronologically, however, the first mention of Titus occurs in Galatians 2:1–3.

> [1] Then after fourteen years I again went up to Yerushalayim, this time with Bar-Nabba; and I took with me **Titus**. [2] I went up in obedience to a revelation, and I explained to them the Good News as I proclaim it among the Gentiles—but privately, to the acknowledged leaders. I did this out of concern that my current or previous work might have been in vain. [3] But they didn't force my Gentile companion **Titus** to undergo *b'rit-milah*.[19] (Galatians 2:1–3)

Titus was a disciple (*talmid*)[20] of Sha'ul the Apostle as well as one of his traveling companions. He was not born Jewish. The place of his birth is not mentioned in Scripture. Since Titus was closely connected with the church of Corinth,[21] it is possible that he might have been born in Corinth. An interesting conjecture is that Titus was Luke's brother.[22] Even though the letter is addressed to Titus, it is a foregone conclusion that this epistle would be read and shared with the Messianic community in Crete.

A true son in the faith we share: Most commentators read "a true son in the faith" to mean that Titus was Sha'ul's convert, though the Scriptures do not explicitly state this. However, I believe that though Titus might have been Sha'ul's convert, the phrase "a true son in the faith" indicates a much stronger and more meaningful relationship, namely that of a rabbi and his disciple (*talmid*). Once the relationship of rabbi (father) and *talmid* (son) is established, the *talmid* would be committed to following his rabbi, as exemplified by Moses and

---

18 Mike Campbell, "Titus." www.BehindTheName.com/name/titus.

19 *B'rit-milah* means "covenant of circumcision."

20 Titus 1:4; 2 Corinthians 8:23.

21 2 Corinthians 2:12; 7:14; 8:16; 8:23.

22 Pastor Chris Bass, "Were Titus and Luke Brothers?" https://PastorChrisBass.wordpress.com/2017/10/09/were-titus-and-luke-brothers.

Joshua, and Elijah and Elisha. This designation is extremely important because by using the term "son" in the sense of *talmid*, it would be understood that Titus was appropriately trained and granted the authority to be Sha'ul's apostolic delegate and ultimate decision-maker for the Messianic community of Crete.[23]

Grace and *shalom*: A common salutation that appears at least a dozen times in Sha'ul's epistles. Some examples can be found in Romans 1:7; 1 Corinthians 1:3; and 1 Timothy 1:2.

Grace / *chesed*: Believers have received an unmerited gift that flows from God's grace (*chesed*). *Chesed* appears 190 times in the *Tanakh* and its Greek cognate *charis* appears 156 times in the *Brit Chadashah*, including four times in the letter to Titus (1:4, 2:11, 3:7, 3:15). In Titus, *chesed* can be understood in a variety of ways. It can be defined as giving oneself fully, with love and compassion. Yeshua's redemption of humanity is the ultimate expression of God's grace, and God's *chesed* is personified as a teacher that instructs a child in the way of righteousness (2:11). God's *chesed* is the active presence of the *Ruach HaKodesh*, which sustains a believer until Yeshua's return (3:7).

Shalom – שָׁלוֹם: Used both as a greeting and farewell, "shalom" carries with it the concept of peace, prosperity, harmony, and well-being. The word "shalom" appears 236 times in the *Tanakh*, and its Greek cognate *eirēnē* appears 92 times in the *Brit Chadashah*.

For followers of Yeshua, shalom is the peace, soundness, health, freedom from worry and the tranquil state of a soul assured of its salvation[24] "that comes through the healing works and forgiving words of Yeshua (See Acts 10:36)."[25] Yeshua imparts to those who trust in him a shalom that surpasses our human understanding.

> Don't worry about anything; on the contrary, make your requests known to God by prayer and petition, with thanksgiving. [7]Then God's *shalom*, passing all understanding, will keep your hearts and minds safe in union with the Messiah Yeshua. (Phil. 4:6–7; cf. Jn. 14:27, 16:33)

---

23 For a more in-depth study of the significance of this relationship, see the essay "Rabbis and Their *Talmidim*."

24 "G1515 – Eirēnē – *Strong's Greek Lexicon* (KJV)."
https://www.BlueLetterBible.org/lexicon/g1515/kjv/tr/0-1.

25 Quinn, *The Anchor Bible*, 75.

Another cogent example of God's shalom is Yosef's response to Pharaoh regarding the interpretation of his troubling dreams. God would answer him with a peaceful explanation and satisfactory solution to avert the coming crisis (Gen. 41:16).

.‫טז וַיַּעַן יוֹסֵף אֶת-פַּרְעֹה לֵאמֹר בִּלְעָדָי אֱלֹהִים יַעֲנֶה אֶת-שְׁלוֹם פַּרְעֹה‬

[16] Yosef answered Pharaoh, "It isn't in me. God will give Pharaoh an answer that will set his mind at peace."

Verses 5–9

[5] The reason I left you in Crete was so that you might attend to the matters still not in order and appoint congregation leaders in each city—those were my instructions. [6] A leader must be blameless, husband to one wife, with believing children who do not have a reputation for being wild or rebellious. [7] For an overseer, as someone entrusted with God's affairs, must be blameless—he must not be self-willed or quick-tempered, he must not drink excessively, get into fights or be greedy for dishonest gain. [8] On the contrary, he must be hospitable, devoted to good, sober-mindedness, uprightness, holiness and self-control. [9] He must hold firmly to the trustworthy Message that agrees with the doctrine; so that by his sound teaching he will be able to exhort and encourage, and also to refute those who speak against it.

Verse 5

My instructions: Sha'ul writes this epistle to Titus to remind him that he left him in Crete so he (Titus) could oversee and complete the organization of the Messianic synagogues, teach sound doctrine to address the divisions being created by the "Circumcision Party," establish the criteria for godly living, and appoint elders and leaders in each city.

Verses 6–7

[6] A leader must be blameless, husband to one wife, with believing children who do not have a reputation for being wild or rebellious. [7] For an overseer, as someone entrusted with God's affairs, must be blameless—he must not be self-willed or quick-

tempered, he must not drink excessively, get into fights or be greedy for dishonest gain.

The character traits and the function of an elder as found in the Letter to Titus are rooted in the *Tanakh*. In Exodus 18, the attributes of the chosen men are trustworthiness, fear of God, and honesty. In Numbers 11, it is the spirit of God, i.e., divine inspiration, that makes a man a member of the elders' council (cf. Judges. 3:10, 6:34, etc.). In Deuteronomy 1, intellectual capacity—wisdom, understanding and knowledge—makes a man fit to judge.[26] Here in verses 6–9, Sha'ul explains the spiritual qualifications for a leader; these are amplified in 2:1–10. First, he explores the domestic sphere of life, noting two aspects of behavior. As in 1 Timothy 3:2, the first matter of concern is the prospective leader's marriage. The second is his reputation as a father.[27]

A leader: The leadership structure for first-century Messianic congregations parallels the pattern found in first-century Jewish synagogues.[28] The synagogue, unlike the Temple priesthood, was a lay institution. No clergy mediated between the people and their God. *Torah* study and prayer were virtues to be cultivated by every Israelite, and positions of leadership in the synagogue were open to all, including women.[29] Since its establishment, people's lives have revolved around the institution of the synagogue, because it served as an amalgamation of three separate institutions: a prayer-house, a study-hall or school, and a community center.

The congregations in Crete would naturally adopt the Jewish synagogue model and leadership structure. For a synagogue to properly function, its leaders must be qualified. That is why, because of their importance and influence, Sha'ul emphasized that Titus was to choose leaders who would not only teach God's Word but also model the conduct and character traits as set forth in Scriptures. Here the concern is chiefly about character and conduct in general. Thus, the concern throughout the passage is on observable behavior, obviously in contrast to that of the "opponents" described in 1:10–16.[30]

---

26 "Elder." https://www.JewishVirtualLibrary.org/elder.

27 Philip H. Towner, *The Letters to Timothy and Titus.*

28 See the essay "A Brief History of the Synagogue."

29 Shaye J. D. Cohen, "The Temple and the Synagogue," in The Cambridge History of Judaism: Vol. 3: The Early Roman Period, 304.

30 Gordon D. Fee, 1 & 2 Timothy, Titus.

A leader of the synagogue is called an elder (Hebrew זָקֵן, *zaken*). The prevalent Greek word used for *zaken* in the LXX is *presbyteros*. The concept of the "Elders of the people of Israel" first emerges in Exodus 3:16:

> [16] Go, gather the **leaders** of Isra'el[31] together, and say to them, '*ADONAI*, the God of your fathers, the God of Avraham, Yitz'chak and Ya'akov, has appeared to me and said, "I have been paying close attention to you and have seen what is being done to you in Egypt.

In Numbers 11, the seventy elders receive the *Ruach HaKodesh* (Holy Spirit), which empowers them to assist Moses in "managing" the children of Israel:

> [16] *ADONAI* said to Moshe, "Bring me seventy of the **leaders** of Isra'el, people you recognize as leaders of the people and officers of theirs. Bring them to the tent of meeting and have them stand there with you. [17] I will come down and speak with you there, and I will take some of the Spirit which rests on you and put it on them. Then they will carry the burden of the people along with you, so that you won't carry it yourself alone. (Numbers 11:16–17)

The first time in the New Testament the word "elder" specifically refers to a leader in a Messianic synagogue is in Acts 20:17 and is rendered *presbyteros*. It is important to note that the same *presbyteros* mentioned in verse 17 are called *episkopos* in verse 28.

> [17] But he did send from Miletus to Ephesus, summoning the **elders** [*presbyteros*] of the Messianic community…[28] "Watch out for yourselves, and for all the flock in which the *Ruach HaKodesh* has placed you as **leaders** [*episkopos*], to shepherd God's Messianic community, which he won for himself at the cost of his own Son's blood. (Acts 20:17, 28)

Most scholars conclude that the words *presbyteros* and *episkopoi* are used interchangeably. The Letter to Titus also uses these words

---

31 "Leaders" is normally rendered *zeqenim*, but in Hebrew, when one noun precedes another, the spelling of the first noun changes. The grammatical rule is called *smichut*. In this verse, "leaders of Israel" is rendered *ziknai' Yisrael*.

interchangeably. In his article, "The Structured Ministry of the Church in the Pastoral Epistles," Joseph A. Fitzmeyer, adds

> In pre-Christian Judaism, too, *presbyteros* denoted "elders," for members of local councils in various towns (LXX: Joshua 20:4; Ruth 4:2; 2 Esdras 10:14; Judith 8:10; 10:6, Hebrew *zikanim)*, [and] also for members of a group in the Sanhédrin, along with the chief priests and scribes. It was undoubtedly from this Jewish ground that the title was taken over by Christians (Acts 11:30; 15:2, 21:18) and given a further nuance when it became the title of those with a function in the structured Christian ministry; hence my translation *presbyteros.*[32]

Blameless: A legal term indicating a person who is above reproach who cannot be charged with an accusation; cf. 1 Corinthians 1: 8; Colossians 1:22; 1 Timothy 3:10.

Husband to one wife: The first matter of concern is the prospective leader's marriage, as is also found in 1 Timothy 3:2. The phrase translated "faithful to his wife" (literally "husband of one wife") describes fidelity within marriage and does not specifically address polygamy or remarriage.[33] Marriage was an important qualification because of the emphasis on family (Genesis 1:28), though some early apocalyptic communities advocated celibacy or separation from one's spouse after the commandment to procreate had been fulfilled (1QSa 1.6–13; 1QM 7.2–4).[34]

> The first positive commandment of the Bible, according to rabbinic interpretation (Maimonides, "Minyan ha-Mizwot," 212), is that concerning the propagation of the human species (Gen. 1:28). It is thus considered the duty of every Israelite to marry as early in life as possible. Eighteen years is the age set by the Rabbis (Ab. v. 24); and any one remaining unmarried after his twentieth year is said to be cursed by God Himself (Kid. 29b). Some urge that children should marry as soon as they reach the age of puberty, *i.e.*, the fourteenth year (*Sanh.* 76b); and R. Hisda attributed his mental superiority to

---

32 Joseph A. Fitzmyer, "The Structured Ministry of the Church in the Pastoral Epistles."
   www.jstor.org/stable/43725325.
33 Towner, *Letters.*
34 Levine and Brettler, *Jewish Annotated New Testament*, 398–399.

the fact that he was married when he was but sixteen years old (Kid. *l.c.*). It was, however, strictly forbidden for parents to give their children in marriage before they had reached the age of puberty (*Sanh.* 76b). A man who, without any reason, refused to marry after he had passed his twentieth year was frequently compelled to do so by the court. To be occupied with the study of the *Torah* was regarded as a plausible reason for delaying marriage, but only in very rare instances was a man permitted to remain in celibacy all his life. (Yeb. 63b; Maimonides, "Yad," Ishut, xv. 2, 3; Shulhan 'Aruk, Eben ha-'Ezer, 1, 1–4; see Celibacy.)[35]

With believing children who do not have a reputation for being wild or rebellious: The reputation of the leader's children was equally important, since the behavior of the children was seen as a reflection of the father's leadership abilities.

Someone entrusted with God's affairs: Leaders represented their fellow citizens in local matters. Their functions are best exemplified by the pertinent laws of Deuteronomy, which directed the city elders to be involved in five areas: (1) blood redemption (19:12); (2) expiation of murder by an unknown culprit (21:3, 6); (3) the rebellious son (21:19); (4) defamation of a virgin (22:15); and (5) levirate (25:9). All these cases deal with protection of the family and local patriarchal interests.

He must not be self-willed: Arrogant.

Or quick-tempered: Easily irritated so that he has an angry disposition.

He must not drink excessively: See comments in chapter 2:3 regarding "older men."

Get into fights: In the sense of being a bully.

Or be greedy for dishonest gain: Fixated on money. See 1 Timothy 3:8; 1 Peter 5:2.

---

35 "Marriage Laws." https://www.JewishEncyclopedia.com/articles/10435-marriage-laws.

Verse 8

[8] On the contrary, he must be hospitable, devoted to good, sober-mindedness, uprightness, holiness, and self-control.

On the contrary: In contrast to the negative traits just listed above, Sha'ul now includes these positive traits leaders must exhibit.

He must be hospitable: The *mitzvah* of hospitality (*hakhnasat orchim*; literally "bringing in of strangers") was a foundational part of Jewish culture. The first examples of *hakhnasat orchimin* in the *Torah* are Abraham providing three strangers with water and food (Gen. 18:1–5) and Rebecca showing hospitality to Abraham's servant, whom he had sent on a journey to find a wife for his son Isaac (Gen. 24:28–32).

Yeshua emphasizes the importance of hospitality in the *mashal* (parable) of The Sheep and the Goats (Mt. 25:31–46). In Hebrews 13:2, Sha'ul reminds believers to never neglect the *mitzvah* of *hakhnasat orchimin*: "Let brotherly friendship continue; [2] but don't forget to be friendly to outsiders; for in so doing, some people, without knowing it, have entertained angels."

Devoted to good: Committed to being a positive role model and example of what it means to be a godly leader and husband.

Sober-mindedness: Self-restraint, to control one's passions by offering one's body as a living sacrifice (Rom. 12:1–4). This expression is also found in 2:2, 5.

Uprightness: A *tzadik* is one who leads a pure, exemplary life by keeping God's *mitzvot*. *Tzadik* is derived from the verb *tzedek*, "to do good," derived from the word *zakah*, "clear, pure." This concept has its basis in Deuteronomy 16:20: "Justice (*tzedek*), only justice (*tzedek*), you must pursue; so that you will live and inherit the land ADONAI your God is giving you."

Holiness: Similar to a *tzadik*, *chasid* is derived from the word *chesed*, "loving kindness." A *chasid* is one who has not been defiled by habitual sin—a pious person with a compassionate heart who engages in acts of loving kindness such as charity and benevolence (*Gemilut Chasadim*).

And self-control: Referred to in 1:8; 2:2, 4, 5. See comments on 2:2.

Verse 9

[9] He must hold firmly to the trustworthy Message that agrees with the doctrine; so that by his sound teaching he will be able to exhort and encourage, and also to refute those who speak against it.

Trustworthy Message ... doctrine / sound teaching: The term "sound teaching" (doctrine) appears regularly in the Pastoral epistles (1 Tim. 1:10; 6:3; 2 Tim. 1:13; 4:3; Titus 1:9, 13; 2:2, 8). This term can be defined as spiritually healthy teaching based on the revealed will of God as presented in the *Tanakh*. The emphasis on maintaining sound doctrine/teaching is referred to throughout the *Brit Chadashah* in a variety of ways: The "apostles' doctrine"; the "doctrine which was delivered you"; and the "doctrine of Christ" (Acts 2:42; Rom. 6:17; 2 John 1:9, KJV).

Sound teaching (doctrine) "is a medical metaphor referring to the 'healthiness' of teaching found in the Gospel and stands in opposition to the 'sickly craving' (1 Tim. 6:3–5); (NIV, "unhealthy interest") of those whose 'teaching will spread like gangrene' (2 Tim. 2:17)."[36] For Sha'ul, the will of God (sound doctrine) is fully revealed through Messiah Yeshua (Rom. 6:17; 1 Cor. 11:23, 15:3; Gal 1:16). Furthermore, the revelation of the will of God can be contrasted with the revelations of the "false teachers." The revealed will of God in Messiah Yeshua is to be transmitted by Yeshua's *talmidim* from generation to generation.

Verses 10–16

[10] For there are many, especially from the Circumcision faction, who are rebellious, who delude people's minds with their worthless and misleading talk. [11] They must be silenced; because they are upsetting entire households by teaching what they have no business teaching and doing it for the sake of dishonest gain. [12] Even one of the Cretans' own prophets has said, "Cretans are always liars, evil brutes, lazy gluttons"—[13] and it's true! For this reason, you must be severe when you rebuke those who have followed this false teaching, so that they

---

36 Fee, 1 & 2 Timothy, Titus.

will come to be sound in their trust [14] and no longer pay attention to Judaistic myths or to the commands of people who reject the truth.

Verse 10

The Circumcision faction: One of the reasons it was imperative that Sha'ul establish his God-given authority to send Titus to Crete was to establish that Titus, as his *talmid*, was well qualified to mediate the conflicts and sharp divisions within the burgeoning Messianic community.

The *Brit Chadashah* contains multiple references to "those of the circumcision."[37]

> On one level, by synecdoche, this simply refers to those who practice circumcision and adhere to other religious customs such as food laws or Sabbath observance, that is, ethnic Jews. On another level it may denote Judaizers, that is, those who insist that Christians must still abide by Jewish customs such as these just mentioned, people whose teaching Paul fiercely opposed (Gal. 2:11–14) and the Jerusalem Council decisively rejected (Acts 15).[38]

Many people who read the New Testament assume that "Circumcision Faction" refers only to non-believing Jews. It is important to keep in mind, as Köstenberger points out, that in the New Testament the traditional Jewish community and the Messianic believers who adhered to the *strict* observance of rabbinic traditions were *both* referred to as the "Circumcision Party."[39]

In *A Commentary on the Jewish Roots of Acts*, Joseph Shulam posits that the members of the Circumcision Faction may refer to those with Pharisaic affiliation, or possibly Jewish converts whose zeal for their newly embraced tradition expressed itself—among other ways—in demand that Gentiles who wish to attach themselves to Judaism become full proselytes rather than remain God-fearers.[40] Members of the Circumcision Faction also included non-Jews who were Yeshua followers who never formally converted to Judaism.

---

37 Acts 10:45; 11:2; Rom. 4:12; Gal. 2:12; Col 4:11.
38 Köstenberger, *Commentary on 1–2 Timothy and Titus.*
39 Köstenberger, *Commentary on 1–2 Timothy and Titus.*
40 Le Cornu and Shulam, *A Commentary*, 608.

The principal conflict in the Letter to Titus existed *within* the Messianic synagogues themselves and was between believers (both Jews and non-Jews) who were oriented toward a stricter adherence to the practices of traditional Judaism for any believer—regardless of ethnic background—and the Jewish and non-Jewish believers who, like Sha'ul, opposed the **strict** application of Jewish customs for gentile converts.[41]

There also existed, within the Messianic Circumcision Party, a subgroup of native-born Cretans who were primarily "Gnosticizing Judaists who as professed Christians sought to infiltrate the churches with their misguided teachings." Fred Gealy posits that they were non-Jews who were attracted to Jewish practices and sought to retain them as obligatory,[42] while Thomas Oden says these Cretan Gnostics were Jewish.[43] Jerome Quinn calls these groups Saul and Titus' "mob of competitors."[44] Thus, the juggernaut and root of the conflict in the Messianic synagogues was how the nascent and emerging Messianic Jewish community in Crete could concretely show that believing in Yeshua of Nazareth as the promised *Mashiach* was consistent with normative Judaism without necessarily embracing all the "Traditions of the Elders."

Verses 12–14

[12] Even one of the Cretans' own prophets has said, "Cretans are always liars, evil brutes, lazy gluttons"—[13] and it's true! For this reason, you must be severe when you rebuke those who have followed this false teaching, so that they will come to be sound in their trust [14] and no longer pay attention to Judaistic myths or to the commands of people who reject the truth.

Cretans are always liars: Simply put, Rav Sha'ul is saying that the native-born Cretans who were promoting incorrect doctrine, were, in essence, not telling the truth—hence they were "liars." To emphasize his point, he quotes the poet Epimenides, a sixth-century B.C.E. native of Crete, who was revered by the Cretans. In Greek literature "to Cretanize" meant to lie.[45]

---

41 Titus 1:10; Sha'ul's opposition is recorded in the Book of Galatians.
42 Gaebelein, Douglas and Polcyn, *Expositor's Bible Commentary*, 432.
43 Thomas C. Oden, *First and Second Timothy and Titus*, 9.
44 Quinn, *The Anchor Bible*, 15.
45 *Zondervan NIV Study Bible*, 1851.

You must be severe when you rebuke those who have followed this false teaching: Titus is exhorted to find good leaders, but also to expose and root out those causing divisions and confusion. False teachers and their followers must be exposed, called to account, and dealt with.

So that they will come to be sound in their trust: The purpose of rebuking those caught up in false teaching is not to punish them but to correct them and turn them to sound doctrine.

Judaistic myths: Fenton Hort aptly says, "The phrase is undoubtedly obscure to us, and cannot well be explained,"[46] but there are various opinions as to the meaning of the phrase "Judaistic myths" and its related phrase "stupid controversies, genealogies, quarrels and fights about the *Torah*."[47] Marc Hirshman from the Hebrew University of Jerusalem advocates, "In the pastoral letter to Titus, Paul is said to have warned the Cretans from heeding 'Jewish myths and human commandments' (Titus 1:14). It would seem the author is warning the audience against the Jewish misunderstanding of Scripture on two fronts, *aggadah* and *halakhah*, interpretation and observance."[48] A parallel verse can be found in Titus 3:9, "But avoid stupid controversies, genealogies, quarrels and fights about the *Torah*; because they are worthless and futile."

Verses 15–16

[15] To all who are themselves pure, everything is pure. But to those who are defiled and without trust, nothing is pure—even their minds and consciences have been defiled. [16] They claim to know God, but with their actions they deny him. They are detestable and disobedient; they have proved themselves unfit to do anything good.

Pure: The concept of purity had a moral and an ethical dimension that was embedded in the *Torah*. As a Pharisee, Sha'ul was quite familiar with the notion of the purity of heart, which manifests itself in righteous behavior, observable in both the private and public sector. The Pharisees had a positive concern for purity; it was better to be pure.[49]

---

46 F. J. A. Hort, *Judaistic Christianity: A Course of Lectures*, 130–146.

47 For a more in-depth study of the significance of Jewish myths, see the essay "*Torah* Controversies."

48 Marc Hirshman, "Origen's View of 'Jewish Fables' in Genesis," in Emmanouela Grypeou and Helen Spurling, *The Exegetical Encounter Between Jews and Christians in Late Antiquity*, 245–254.

49 Jacob Neusner, *In Quest of the Historical Pharisees*, 405.

This notion was also of particular concern for Yeshua followers.[50] The inclusion of non-Jews in the Messianic community was a specific concern for members of the Circumcision Faction, as Gentiles were considered impure. Table fellowship with non-Jews was a major issue and had been brought to the Jerusalem Council's attention when Kefa (Peter) went to Cornelius' home.

> [1] The emissaries and the brothers throughout Y'hudah heard that the *Goyim* had received the word of God; [2] but when Kefa went up to Yerushalayim, the members of the Circumcision faction criticized him, [3] saying, "You went into the homes of uncircumcised men and even ate with them!" (Acts 11:1–3)

Kefa (Peter) had addressed their concern, explaining how in a vision a voice from heaven had instructed him to go to Cornelius' home and not to consider him unclean, saying, "Stop treating as unclean what God has made clean" (Acts 11:9). We know from Acts 10:25–29 that the unclean or impure animals Kefa had seen represented people, not food, when he tells Cornelius:

> You are well aware that for a man who is a Jew to have close association with someone who belongs to another people, or to come and visit him, is something that just isn't done. But God has shown me not to call any person common or unclean.

Upon hearing that Cornelius and his family had received the Holy Spirit, just as they had, those in the Council rejoiced, realizing God had granted the Gentiles salvation (Acts 11:18). But subscribing to the false teachings of the Circumcision Faction, which sought to make the Gentile believers "clean" through circumcision, showed their own hearts were not pure in accepting others or understanding God's grace. Insisting on outward actions can only defile a person and prevent them from becoming inwardly pure, rendering them "unfit to do anything good." Their teachings and practices nullify the message of the *Besorah* (Gospel), which is intended for "the Jew first and then the Greek" (Rom. 1:16).

---

50 Jacob Neusner, *Judaism*, 57–59.

CHAPTER TWO

Verses 1–10

[1] But you, explain what kind of behavior goes along with sound teaching. [2] Tell the older men to be serious, sensible, self-controlled, and sound in their trust, love, and perseverance. [3] Likewise, tell the older women to behave the way people leading a holy life should. They shouldn't be slanderers or slaves to excessive drinking. They should teach what is good, [4] thus training the younger women to love their husbands and children, [5] to be self-controlled and pure, to take good care of their homes and submit to their husbands. In this way, God's message will not be brought into disgrace.

[6] Similarly, urge the young men to be self-controlled, [7] and in everything set them an example yourself by doing what is good. When you are teaching, have integrity and be serious; [8] let everything you say be so wholesome that an opponent will be put to shame because he will have nothing bad to say about us.

[9] Tell slaves to submit to their masters in everything, to give satisfaction without talking back [10] or pilfering. On the contrary, they should demonstrate complete faithfulness always, so that in every way they will make the teaching about God our Deliverer more attractive.

This section addresses the topic of godly behavior within one's household that conforms to sound teaching (2:1–10). Many congregations met in homes (Rom. 16:5; 1 Cor. 16:19; Philem. 2; cf. Col. 4:45), and the leadership of the early congregations "seem to have normally been drawn from the functioning heads of the households, whose own family life along with the members of his family was to be exemplary."[51] Most commentators place the attributes listed in 2:2–10 under the category of "Household Codes." As a Pharisee, Sha'ul would have been familiar with many of the domestic household codes (*Ma'aseh*) of the Pharisaic patriarchal figures Gamaliel, Simeon b. Gamaliel, and Hillel, who are lauded in

---

51 Danny Wade Russell, "Congregational Leadership Development Through Mentorships." https://DigitalCommons.georgefox.edu/dmin/82.

the *Mishnah*'s *Ma'asim*.[52] Similar lists of "Household Codes" appear in Ephesians 5:21–6:9 and Colossians 3:18–4:1. Titus can fulfill this task through his teaching as well as by modeling godly behavior, serving as a living example of "sound teaching."

Verse 1

But you, explain what kind of behavior goes along with sound teaching.

But you, explain: Sha'ul's additional instruction to Titus, his designated emissary, is to present and explain the significance of sound teaching[53] to various groups. This careful transmission (*Mesorah*) of sound teaching from one generation to another is frequently mentioned in the writings of Sha'ul, the prime example being 1 Corinthians 15:3: "For among the first things I passed on to you was what I also received, namely this: the Messiah died for our sins, in accordance with what the *Tanakh* says..."

This is my reconstruction of the chain of transmission (*mesorah*) that is reflected in the Letter to Titus: Yeshua revealed himself to Sha'ul on the road to Damascus. Sha'ul carefully transmitted this revelation to his *talmidim* (disciples), one of them being Titus. Titus delivers (transmits) the "sound teaching" that he received from Sha'ul to the *Ziqeneem* (elders) in Crete who, in turn, transmit these revelations to the members of the Cretan messianic community which includes younger men, younger women, and slaves.[54]

Verse 2

Tell the older men to be serious, sensible, self-controlled, and sound in their trust, love, and perseverance.

Tell the older men ... [and older women in vs. 3]: Philip Towner represents the common consensus when he states that the terms "older men" and "older women" refer to chronological age and do not mean

---

52 Neusner, *In Quest*, 184.
53 Often translated as "sound doctrine."
54 For a more in-depth study of the significance of mesorah, see the essay *"Mesorah."*

"elders" in the sense of leadership as in 1:6 (cf. 1 Tim 5:1).[55] I disagree and believe Sha'ul is specifying that Titus is to teach the leaders, both men and women.

The term **"older"** that is employed in 2:2–5 is *presbytēs* (male) and *presbytis* (female)—both derivatives of *presbyteros*, which is utilized in 1:6. The context of these passages (2:2–5) indicates that *presbytēs* refers to leaders, not senior citizens. In general, the leaders of the synagogue, based on their life experience, would tend to be expected to lead by modeling godly behavior in their households. In Jewish contexts, elders (usually older men) were respected for piety and wisdom (Exod. 3.16; Num. 11.16; see also Judith 8.10, Sus. 1.5; Philo, *On the Contemplative Life*, Book 67); in the *Mishnah* the elders are the bearers of the tradition (Avot 1); the New Testament frequently lists elders with chief priests (Mt. 16.21; Lk. 9.22).[56]

As noted at 1:6, *Torah* study and prayer were virtues every Israelite was to cultivate, and, as a lay institution, leadership positions in the synagogue were open to all, including women.

To be serious: This is a term which means not to have a diminished mental capacity due to the consumption of too much wine; to be sober.

Sensible: To merit respect because of personal character and conduct.

Self-controlled: Self-control or temperance, was one of the four cardinal virtues advocated by both Jewish and Gentile writers (Aristotle, Homer, Philo, Josephus).[57] The admonition to be self-controlled is also given to the younger women as well as to the younger men.

And sound in their trust: Men should be well-grounded in the knowledge of what constitutes sound teaching as well as the ability to impart this knowledge to the members of their household in a trustworthy manner.

---

55 Towner, *Letters.*
56 Levine and Brettler, *Jewish Annotated New Testament*, 398–399.
57 David H. Stern, *Jewish New Testament Commentary: A Companion Volume to the Jewish New Testament*, 400.

Love: This is the Greek word *agape*, which can be defined as the highest form of love, describing God's unconditional love for mankind and mankind's reciprocal love for God. We love God because he first loved us (1 John 4:19).

And perseverance: The strength of character to remain patient, loyal and faithful to God during life's storms.

Verses 3–5

[3] Likewise, tell the older women to behave the way people leading a holy life should. They shouldn't be slanderers or slaves to excessive drinking. They should teach what is good, [4] thus training the younger women to love their husbands and children, [5] to be self-controlled and pure, to take good care of their homes and submit to their husbands. In this way, God's message will not be brought into disgrace.

Reflective of Sha'ul's Pharisaic background is his understanding of a woman's leadership role and influence in the community. According to Neusner, the importance of women leaders was embraced by Pharisaism. Consequently, in the Pharisaic rite, women enjoyed full personhood.[58]

Likewise … the older women: The older women, particularly as leaders, are expected to conduct themselves in a similar manner as the older men.

Behave the way people leading a holy life should: To be similarly reverent and devout in their deportment as becomes those engaged in sacred service.[59] In other words, to live one's life as a person who serves God in the temple and considers every facet of life as holy. In Hellenistic Greek Jewish culture, the term can suggest an internal quality as well as external deportment.[60]

They shouldn't be slanderers: Prohibition against *Lashon Harah*[61] ("evil tongue"), which James emphasizes as "the tongue is a fire, a world of wickedness. The tongue is so placed in our body that it

---

58 Neusner, *Judaism*, 58–59.
59 *The Amplified Bible*, 1954.
60 Quinn, *The Anchor Bible*, 118.
61 Famous book on slander and gossip by the *Chofetz Chaim*.

defiles every part of it, setting ablaze the whole of our life; and it is set on fire by *Gei-Hinnom* itself" (James 3:6).

Or slaves to excessive drinking: See comments on 2:2.

They should teach what is good: Godly behavior and principles are taught, not instinctive, and children need to be trained to do good. An older woman needs to be a positive role and example of what it means to be a godly wife.

Training the younger women: Notice that Titus does not directly teach the younger women. He assigns this task to the older women. This is due to Jewish laws of *Yichud* ("gender separation"), which in general prevent males from having direct contact with females who are not their spouse or immediate family members.[62]

Love their husbands and children: To be devoted to the well-being to the members of one's family. In a culture of predominantly arranged marriages, the wife's role was central in setting the tone for a peaceful, loving home.

To be self-controlled: See comments on 2:2.

And pure: Chastity and the purity of actions that are the outflow of purity of heart, mind and body. To the pure, all things are pure. See comments on 1:9.

To take good care of their homes: The key word here, *oikourgos*, is used in the sense of having compassion and acting kindly toward all the members of one's household, including servants (cf. 1 Thes. 5:15; Eph. 4:28).

And submit to their husbands: The cultural norm of the Hellenistic and Jewish world was that wives should submit to their husbands. "Submission (*hypotassô*) implies a recognition of and support of a husband's authority."[63] Sha'ul gives the theological basis for submission in Eph. 5:22–33, Col. 3:18–19 and 1 Pet. 3:1–7.

In this way, God's message will not be brought into disgrace: Those of the Circumcision Faction and other opponents of the Sound

---

62 For a further explanation, refer to *The Passionate Torah: Sex and Judaism*, ed. Danya Ruttenberg.
63 Hulitt Gloer and Perry Leon Stepp, *Reading Paul's Letters to Individuals: A Literary and Theological Commentary on Paul's Letters to Philemon, Titus, and Timothy*, 109.

Teaching as taught by Sha'ul, Titus, Apollos and others are always looking to point out any inconsistent behavior of Yeshua followers to try to discredit the message of the Gospel.

Verses 6–8

Similarly, urge the young men to be self-controlled, [7] and in everything set them an example yourself by doing what is good. When you are teaching, have integrity and be serious; [8] let everything you say be so wholesome that an opponent will be put to shame because he will have nothing bad to say about us.

Similarly ... young men: The same basic principles of godly conduct given to young women also apply to young men.

To be self-controlled: Titus is to call young men (presumably 20-30 years of age; *TDNT* 4:897)—who might tend to lack restraint—to a level-headed, disciplined life. This self-mastery involves "control of temper and tongue, of ambition and ... bodily appetites."[64]

In everything set them an example yourself by doing what is good: Titus' example must show evidence of the "good works" that characterize a godly life. Like his father in the faith, he is to be an imitator of the Messiah.

- Try to imitate me, even as I myself try to imitate the Messiah. (1 Corinthians 11:1)
- Brothers, join in imitating me, and pay attention to those who live according to the pattern we have set for you. (Philippians 3:17)
- So, imitate God, as his dear children... (Ephesians 5:1)

In Judaism, "the life of the rabbi was itself Torah." [65] Likewise, in Hellenistic culture, the teacher was to be a living demonstration of his teaching.

Let everything you say be so wholesome that an opponent will be put to shame because he will have nothing bad to say about us: See comments on 2:5. The behavior or misbehavior of individuals is often seen as a reflection on the whole community.

---

64 Köstenberger, *Commentary on 1–2 Timothy and Titus.*
65 W. D. Davies, *The Setting of the Sermon on the Mount*, 455.

Verses 9–10

Tell slaves to submit to their masters in everything, to give satisfaction without talking back or pilfering. On the contrary, they should demonstrate complete faithfulness always, so that in every way they will make the teaching about God our Deliverer more attractive.

Slaves: Sha'ul is not endorsing slavery but addresses it as a given reality. By the first century C.E., Jews lived various existences in the Roman Empire and in Rome itself. Though the exact number and ratio of each is not known, many Jews under Roman rule were slaves. Some were lifetime slaves, but most were indentured or slaves for a set period. Once they had served their time, they were freed through a process called manumission. Many of Rome's Jews were this type of freed slaves. In fact, some were even made Roman citizens upon manumission, and there was a large population of Jews who were citizens of Rome in the first century C.E.

It stands to reason that some of the slaves who were members of the Messianic community in Crete were also Jewish—either lifetime slaves or indentured servants, possibly even freed slaves. Slaves are also mentioned as being members of the Messianic communities at Corinth (1 Cor. 12:13), Galatia (Gal. 6:5), and Colossi (Col. 3:11). 1 Cor. 7:22 likely alludes to freed slaves:

> [22] For the one who was a slave when called to faith in the Lord is the Lord's freed person; similarly, the one who was free when called is Christ's slave.

Nasrallah elaborates:

> Thus it may not be coincidental that in a letter to Corinth we find the only use in the New Testament of the technical term "freed-person" (*apeleutheros*, 7:22). Some freedmen in Corinth held high civic positions and the Forum was marked by the benefactions of ex-slaves. Paul's words "Let … those … who buy [be] as though they had no possessions, and those who deal with the world as though they had no dealings with it" (7:29–31) would have been particularly thought-provoking to Corinthians-in-Christ in an urban setting in

which buying and dealings with the world were central to civic identity—and in which having been bought and later manumitted were part of the identity of local elites. (Nasrallah 2013).[66]

Demonstrate complete faithfulness always: Whatever their status, slaves are admonished to serve their masters well, which exemplifies godly behavior.

They will make the teaching about God our Deliverer more attractive: In verse 10, "sound teaching" is compared to an ornament that everyone can see.

The common denominator in Paul's instructions is the importance of the believers' witness to the Gospel in their unbelieving environment: "so that God's message will not be brought into disgrace" (2:5), "so that the opponent will be put to shame because he will have nothing bad to say about us" (2:8), and "so that in every way they will make the teaching about God our Deliverer more attractive" (2:10).[67]

Verses 11–15

For God's grace, which brings deliverance, has appeared to all people. [12] It teaches us to renounce godlessness and worldly pleasures, and to live self-controlled, upright and godly lives now, in this age; [13] while continuing to expect the blessed fulfillment of our certain hope, which is the appearing of the *Sh'khinah* of our great God and the appearing of our Deliverer, Yeshua the Messiah. [14] He gave himself up on our behalf in order to free us from all violation of *Torah* and purify for himself a people who would be his own, eager to do good. [15] These are the things you should say. Encourage and rebuke with full authority; don't let anyone look down on you.

Verses 11–14

These verses discuss the relationship between Sound Teaching, God's grace, and godly living.

---

66 Laura Nasrallah, "Chapter-Length Commentary on 1 Corinthians (Fortress Press)." https://www.academia.edu/7457182/Chapter_length_commentary_on_1_Corinthians_Fortress_Press.
67 Köstenberger, *Commentary on 1–2 Timothy and Titus.*

In this verse, *chesed* means giving oneself fully, with love and compassion. God's *chesed* teaches, delivers and purifies a person from their former way of life, resulting in a desire to do good. Godly behavior ultimately prepares Yeshua's followers for his return. The entire process of redemption is rooted in God's grace, which is a historical reality that will culminate in "the blessed fulfillment of our certain hope, which is the appearing of the *Sh'khinah* of our great God and the appearing of our Deliverer, Yeshua the Messiah (Titus 2:13)."[68]

Verse 15

Encourage and rebuke with full authority; don't let anyone look down on you: It is possible that Titus' credibility was called into question because he was not born Jewish.

CHAPTER THREE

Verses 1–8

Remind people to submit to the government and its officials, to obey them, to be ready to do any honorable kind of work, [2] to slander no one, to avoid quarrelling, to be friendly, and to behave gently towards everyone. [3] For at one time, we too were foolish and disobedient, deceived and enslaved by a variety of passions and pleasures. We spent our lives in evil and envy; people hated us, and we hated each other. [4] But when the kindness and love for mankind of God our Deliverer was revealed, [5] he delivered us. It was not on the ground of any righteous deeds we had done, but on the ground of his own mercy. He did it by means of the *mikveh* of rebirth and the renewal brought about by the *Ruach HaKodesh*, [6] whom he poured out on us generously through Yeshua the Messiah, our Deliverer. [7] He did it so that by his grace we might come to be considered righteous by God and become heirs, with the certain hope of eternal life. [8] You can trust what I have just said, and I want you to speak with confidence about these things, so that those who have put their trust in God may apply themselves to doing good deeds. These are both good in themselves and valuable to the community.

---

68 Gaebelein, Douglas, and Polcyn, *Expositor's Bible Commentary*, 441.

Verses 1–3

Remind people to submit to the government and its officials, to obey them, to be ready to do any honorable kind of work, ² to slander no one, to avoid quarrelling, to be friendly, and to behave gently towards everyone. ³ For at one time, we too were foolish and disobedient, deceived and enslaved by a variety of passions and pleasures.

Remind people to submit to the government and its officials: Jerome D. Quinn states that the reminder to submit "to the government and its officials" is particularly directed to Jewish believers because of the numerous acts of sedition by the Jews against the Roman government.[69]

To slander no one, to avoid quarrelling, to be friendly, and to behave gently towards everyone: Godly behavior is not limited to manifesting itself within the household of faith but should extend itself into the public sector.

For at one time, we too were foolish and disobedient, deceived and enslaved by a variety of passions and pleasures: Looking back on our own misbehaviors should serve as a reminder that we need to forgive others their shortcomings just as we have been forgiven. Col. 3:13; Eph. 4:32.

Verses 4–7

⁴ But when the kindness and love for mankind of God our Deliverer was revealed, ⁵ he delivered us. It was not on the ground of any righteous deeds we had done, but on the ground of his own mercy. He did it by means of the *mikveh* of rebirth and the renewal brought about by the *Ruach HaKodesh*, ⁶ whom he poured out on us generously through Yeshua the Messiah, our Deliverer. ⁷ He did it so that by his grace we might come to be considered righteous by God and become heirs, with the certain hope of eternal life.

⁴ **But when the kindness and love for mankind of God our Deliverer was revealed, ⁵ he delivered us:** The Pharisees embraced the concept of the universal salvation of all mankind.

---

69 For a well-documented article regarding this subject, see Jeff Hays, "Early Jewish Groups, Revolts and Wars Against Rome." **https://factsanddetails.com/world/cat55/sub351/item1383.html**.

It has been maintained that the Pharisees were narrow nationalists, in contrast to the prophets who were universalists. Such a view betrays lack of knowledge of the tannaitic literature and the essence of Pharisaism. The canonization of the prophetic books, Isaiah, Jeremiah, Amos and Micah, making their views fundamental for Judaism, was accomplished by the Pharisees. They were responsible for abolishing the term "House of Yahweh" and substituting the term "Sanctuary." They thereby emphasized that the God of Israel is universal, that no house could contain him, that he is everywhere. The Pharisees were far from being narrow nationalists. They were the first to maintain that anyone, regardless of race, can be converted to Judaism since Judaism is a universal religion.[70]

On the ground of his own mercy: Believers should "remember not to forget" that it is through God's *chesed* that they have been "called out of darkness into his wonderful light" (1 Pet. 2:9).

He did it by means of the *mikveh* of rebirth and the renewal brought about by the *Ruach HaKodesh*, [6] whom he poured out on us generously through Yeshua the Messiah, our Deliverer: The process of rebirth is compared to being immersed in a *mikveh*, a pool of water in which certain Jewish ritual purifications are performed. Renewal brought by the pouring out of the *Ruach HaKodesh* is an allusion to several passages in the *Tanakh*, including Ezekiel 36:24–27 and Joel 3:1–2 (2:28–29 in other translations).

[24] For I will take you from among the nations,
gather you from all the countries,
and return you to your own soil.
[25] Then I will sprinkle clean water on you,
and you will be clean;
I will cleanse you from all your uncleanness
and from all your idols.
[26] I will give you a new heart
and put a new spirit inside you;
I will take the stony heart out of your flesh
and give you a heart of flesh.

---

70 Solomon Zeitlin, "The Pharisees: A Historical Study," in Christine Hayes, ed., *Classic Essays in Early Rabbinic Culture and History*, 107.

27 I will put my Spirit inside you
and cause you to live by my laws,
respect my rulings and obey them.

3 (2:28) After this, I will pour out
my Spirit on all humanity.
Your sons and daughters will prophesy,
your old men will dream dreams, your young men will see visions;
2 (2:29) and also on male and female slaves
in those days I will pour out my Spirit.

He did it so that by his grace we might come to be considered righteous by God and become heirs, with the certain hope of eternal life: Rebirth and renewal are manifestations of God's *chesed*, and they bring a person into right relationship with one's Heavenly Abba.

Verse 8

8 You can trust what I have just said, and I want you to speak with confidence about these things, so that those who have put their trust in God may apply themselves to doing good deeds. These are both good in themselves and valuable to the community.

Sha'ul reminds Titus that his labor in Crete, though difficult, is not in vain. Sha'ul is confident that this is true because this is his personal experience in his endeavors as a *shaliach*. Titus should remain confident and continue to be an example of the blessings of serving Yeshua through acts of loving kindness (*gemilut chasidim*).

Verses 9–11

9 But avoid stupid controversies, genealogies, quarrels and fights about the *Torah*; because they are worthless and futile. **10** Warn a divisive person once, then a second time; and after that, have nothing more to do with him. **11** You may be sure that such a person has been perverted and is sinning: he stands self-condemned.

But avoid stupid controversies, genealogies, quarrels and fights about the *Torah*: Titus is again reminded to stay focused on his teaching, avoiding these distractions. See 1:14–16 notes.

¹⁰ Warn a divisive person once, then a second time; and after that, have nothing more to do with him: Divisive people and those purporting unsound doctrines need to be corrected, but here the principles and processes of Matt.18:15 and Gal. 6:1–3 should be applied, giving them a chance to repent and change. Rejection is necessary if they refuse to repent.

> Moreover, if your brother commits a sin against you, go and show him his fault—but privately, just between the two of you. If he listens to you, you have won back your brother. (Mt. 18:15)

> ¹ Brothers, suppose someone is caught doing something wrong. You who have the Spirit should set him right, but in a spirit of humility, keeping an eye on yourselves so that you won't be tempted too. ² Bear one another's burdens—in this way you will be fulfilling the *Torah's* true meaning, which the Messiah upholds. (Gal. 6:1–3)

Verses 12–15

Sha'ul ends his letter to Titus with some personal notes, including some directives concerning various individuals, and he concludes with greetings and prayer.

¹² When I send Artemas or Tychicus to you. Do your best to come to me in Nicopolis, for I have decided to spend the winter there. ¹³ Do your best to help Zenas the *Torah* expert and Apollos with their arrangements for travelling, so that they will lack nothing. ¹⁴ And have our people learn to apply themselves to doing good deeds that meet genuine needs, so that they will not be unproductive.

¹⁵ All, who are with me, send you greetings. Give our greetings to our friends in the faith. Grace be with you all.

Verse 12

¹² When I send Artemas or Tychicus to you. Do your best to come to me in Nicopolis, for I have decided to spend the winter there:

Aretemas: Little is known about Artemas. He is a possible replacement for Titus because Sha'ul needs Titus to assist him in

Nicopolis.[71] The Orthodox Church in America considers him the Bishop of Lystra and one of the 70 Apostles. Since Artemis, the mother goddess of the earth, was worshiped in Ephesus, his name suggests he may have been a pagan convert from Ephesus.

Tychicus: Another possible replacement for Titus. In Ephesians 6:21 and Colossians 4:7, Sha'ul calls Tychicus a beloved brother and faithful minister in the Lord. Apparently, similar to Titus, Tychicus was one of Sha'ul's emissaries and traveling companions (2 Tim. 4:12). Based on his frequent mention in Scripture, it seems he would be a highly qualified replacement for Titus.

Verse 13

[13] Do your best to help Zenas the *Torah* expert and Apollos with their arrangements for travelling, so that they will lack nothing: Most commentators say the text is unclear as to whether Zenas and Apollos were passing through Crete on their way to another destination, or if they came to Crete with Titus to serve as his assistants. If they were in Crete as Titus' assistants, they certainly would have been able to help Titus deal with the "community controversies" created by the "mob of competitors" regarding the interpretation of the *Torah* and *Tanakh*.

Do your best to help Zenas: There is limited information about the personal life of Zenas except that he is designated as a lawyer (*nomikos*), which could mean an expert in Greek or Roman civil law, but more likely refers to an expert in the *Torah* and Jewish Law. In the *Complete Jewish Bible,* David Stern understands the word "lawyer" as referring to a *Torah* expert.

The *Torah* expert: The commendation of Zenas and Apollos, like that of Titus, is another indication of Sha'ul's choice of educated and capable people to serve as leaders and teachers who could correctly interpret the Scriptures.

---

71 The capital city of the Roman province of Epirus Vetus, in the western part of the modern state of Greece.

> Study *and* be eager *and* do your utmost to present yourself to God approved (tested by trial), a workman who has no cause to be ashamed, correctly analyzing *and* accurately dividing [rightly handling and skillfully teaching] the Word of Truth. (2 Timothy 2:15, AMPC)

Apollos: In contrast, Apollos is frequently mentioned in the New Testament. He is described as well-versed in Scripture and was well-instructed in the way of the Lord Yeshua. Apollos was Jewish and a native of Alexandria, which would endear him to many of the inhabitants of Crete, as much of the population's family origins were Alexandrian. After receiving some theological fine-tuning from Priscilla and Aquila, he was sent to Achaia, where he demonstrated his ability to be a powerful apologist for the Messiahship of Yeshua of Nazareth (Acts 18:24–28).

Sometime later, Apollos traveled to Corinth from Achaia where he met Sha'ul. Subsequently Apollos became an important member of Sha'ul's servant-leadership team.

> After all, what is **Apollos**? What is Sha'ul? Only servants through whom you came to trust. Indeed, it was the Lord who brought you to trust through one of us or through another. I planted the seed, and **Apollos** watered it, but it was God who made it grow. (1 Corinthians 3:5–6)

Since both Apollos and Titus are frequently mentioned in the letters addressed to the Corinthians, it is quite possible they first met in Corinth.

Verse 14

14 And have our people learn to apply themselves to doing good deeds that meet genuine needs, so that they will not be unproductive.

Faith without corresponding acts of loving kindness is unproductive.

Verse 15

[15] **All, who are with me, send you greetings. Give our greetings to our friends in the faith. Grace be with you all. Amen.**

Grace be with you all: This is the fourth time the subject of God's *chesed* is mentioned (cf. 1:4, 2:11, 3:7). Sha'ul ends his letter to Titus by imparting God's love, mercy, and eternal presence to his beloved disciple and all who are with him.

5

RUMINATIONS AND ILLUMINATIONS

POWER FROM ON HIGH –
SHAVUOT, SIVAN 6, 30 C.E.

Introduction

The Book of Acts records one of the most anticipated events in the history of the Kingdom of Heaven. This event took place on *Shavuot,* Sivan 6, 30 C.E. On this particular *Shavuot,* the number of Yeshua's *talmidim,* the 120, increased by 3000 members (Acts 2:41).

Symbolically, the 3000 were a "first-fruits" offering as typified by the wave offering of the *Shtai HaLechem* (the two leavened loaves) that were presented to HaShem[1] in the *Beit HaMikdash.*[2] In my opinion, this first-fruits offering included Jews from Crete who were added to the faith and filled with power from on high and who subsequently brought the Good News of Yeshua to their homeland.

The purpose of this essay is to provide the details of the observance of *Shavuot* in the first century of the Common Era, which will enhance one's understanding of what actually occurred on *Shavuot* – Sivan 6, 30 C.E.!

Shavuot – Sivan 6, 30 c.e.

According to some scholars, approximately 200,000 people went up to Yerushalayim to celebrate *Shavuot.* Yeshua's *talmidim* had been in Yerushalayim since his Triumphal Entry, which took place a week

---

1 See *VahYikrah* 23:15–22; *Bemidbar* 28:26; *Devarim* 16:10.
2 Another name for the Temple. Literally "sanctified" or "holy House" (בֵּית־הַמְּקְדָּשׁ). I am using the Hebrew names for the books of the *Tanakh.* The list of the names can be found at http://www.JewFAQ.org/torah.htm.

before Pesach (Mt. 21:1–6). After Yeshua's resurrection, his *talmidim* spent an additional 40 days with him learning about the principles of the "Kingdom of God" as well as eagerly anticipating being "filled with Power from on High" (Acts 1:1ff). This intense time of discipleship took place during the time known as *Sefirat HaOmer* (Lev. 23:15–16).[3]

Shavuot was one of the *Shalosh Regalim* commonly known as the three Pilgrim Feasts (Ex. 23:14–19; Deut. 16:10–12). The basic requirements of this feast were:

1. To joyfully appear before HaShem in the *Azarah* (the Temple courtyard).

2. To present to HaShem a wave offering of *Shtai HaLechem* with its accompanying offering of two lambs.

3. To present an offering of the Seven Species (Deut. 8:8), wheat being one of the Seven Species.

The Preparation of the Wave Offering

The wheat flour known as *solees* or purified flour was the main ingredient of the *Shtai HaLechem.* The wheat was harvested and prepared a few days before *Shavuot* in the *Azarah.*

The wheat was winnowed, beaten, ground in a mill, and placed through a 13-stage sifting process. The wheat was then mixed with water and leaven and then baked. Each loaf of bread was made individually from its own piece of dough. These details are all found in the *Talmud.*[4]

This preparation process typifies harvesting and gathering in "fruit for eternal life" (Jn. 4:31–38). The world is God's wheat field. Each person is sifted and prepared through their life experiences to enter the Kingdom of God. The two individually prepared loaves that are made

---

3 For a more detailed explanation, see John J. Parsons, "*Sefirat HaOmer.*"
   www.Hebrew4Christians.com/Holidays/Spring_Holidays/Sefirat_HaOmer/sefirat_haomer.html.
4 The best book on the subject is Menachem Moshe Oppen's *A Pictorial Guide to the Korban Mincha,* online at https://HebrewBooks.org/47035. Also refer to *Menachos* 86b (cf. *Tosafos* in *Da'as Zekeinim MiBa'alei Hatosafot to Bamidbar 28:25* and *Rambam* in *Temidim Umusafimi 8:1*).

with *water* and *leaven* represent the body of the *Mashiach*, which is comprised of Jews and Greeks. The term "Greeks" signifies the people groups of the nations. Each member of each group has been redeemed and washed by the regenerating *water* of the *Ruach HaKodesh* (Titus 3:5). Yet at the same time, because each person still lives in their mortal body, each individual struggles with the *leaven* of their sinful nature (Rom. 7:13–25).

The Presentation of the Wave Offering

In between the morning and the afternoon *Korban Tamid*—the continual burnt offering (Ex. 29:38)—the *Shtai HaLechem* were waved twice before HaShem. They were waved in six directions: north, south, east, west, up and down. The first time (*tnufa*) they were waved together with the two live lambs. The lambs were then slaughtered and cut into individual pieces. Then the *Shtai HaLechem* were waved in the same six directions with a piece or pieces of the lambs, which were placed on top of the loaves. The lambs were then burned on the Temple's *mizbayach*.[5]

The wave offering is considered to be a *korban todah* (Lev. 7:12), a thanksgiving offering, which is offered to give thanks to Adonai for rescuing a person from individual disaster such as a sickness or an arduous journey, especially a journey at sea (Ps. 107).

The two wavings of the two loaves and lambs in the six directions typify the following:

1. The two lambs represent that Yeshua has redeemed both Jews and Greeks from personal disaster caused by the wages of sin which is death (Rom. 6:23).

2. The two live lambs represent that the Lamb of God who takes away the sins of the world lives forever (Jn. 11:25).

3. The sacrifice of the lambs represents that the Lamb of God had to suffer to redeem mankind (Isa. 53:1ff).

---

5 *Mizbayah* מִזְבֵּחַ is Hebrew for "altar."

4. The wave offering being a *todah* offering indicates that the Lamb of God is merciful and rescues each of his children from the disaster of darkness into the blessings of his kingdom of marvelous light (1 Pet. 2:9).

The Celebration of *Shavuot* and Acts Chapter Two

Yeshua's *talmidim* were faithful Jews who were obedient to the *Torah* to go up to Yerushalayim to celebrate *Shavuot*. They were gathered together with hundreds of thousands of people in the location the Book of Acts calls the "Place," which in Hebrew is *HaMakom*. The "Place" was the Temple and in particular the Temple courtyard which is known as the *Azarah*.

> The festival of *Shavu'ot* arrived, and the believers all gathered together in one place. (Acts 2:1)

Many verses in the *Tanakh* refer the Temple as *HaMakom*.

> You will bring them in and plant them
> on the mountain, which is your heritage,
> **the place**, *ADONAI*, that you made your abode,
> the sanctuary, *Adonai*, which your hands established. (Ex. 15:17)

> "Three times a year all your men are to appear in the presence of *ADONAI* your God in **the place** which he will choose—at the festival of *matzah*, at the festival of *Shavu'ot* and at the festival of *Sukkot*. They are not to show up before *ADONAI* empty-handed." (Deut. 16:16)

> In the first year of Koresh the king, Koresh the king issued this decree: "Concerning the house of God in Yerushalayim, let the house be rebuilt, the place where they offer sacrifices; and let its foundations be firmly laid. Its height is to be ninety feet and its breadth ninety feet." (Ezra 6:3)

The Temple is also known as the "The House" (*HaBayit)* or "The Mountain of the House" (*Har HaBayit*). The *Talmidim* of Yeshua were seated in one of the study areas of the House, expecting to receive the long-awaited promise of the outpouring of the *Ruach HaKodesh.* Then suddenly the long-awaited outpouring of the *Ruach HaKodesh* descends from *HaShamayim.*[6]

> Suddenly there came a sound from the sky like the roar of a violent wind, and it filled the **whole house** where they were sitting. [3] Then they saw what looked like tongues of fire, which separated and came to rest on each one of them. [4] They were all filled with the *Ruach HaKodesh* and began to talk in different languages, as the Spirit enabled them to speak. (Acts 2:2–4)

Kefa, anointed by the *Ruach,* speaks prophetically to the crowd of people, and 3000 are "cut to the heart" and subsequently saved.[7] Among the 3000 new believers were **Jews from Crete** as well as Jews from the four corners of the earth. They were a type of "first-fruits" wave offering who, after the Feast, returned to their respective homelands "to promote among God's chosen people the trust and knowledge of truth which lead to godliness and which are based on the certain hope of eternal life" (Titus 1:1a–2a).

---

6 *Shamayim* שָׁמַיִם is the Hebrew word for Heaven.
7 Acts 2:5–41.

SHA'UL THE PHARISEE

At the time of Yeshua, "Jews" were not one homogenous religious group but a mix of numerous divergent and conflicting schools of thought, the two major groups being the Sadducees and Pharisees. Germane to the interpretation of Titus is the realization that Sha'ul was a Pharisee. Pinchas Lapide and Peter Stuhlmacher were among the first scholars to acknowledge him as a Pharisee.[8] Daniel Boyarin states, "If we take Paul at his word—and I see no reason not to—he was a member of the Pharisaic wing of first-century Judaism."[9] He himself claimed to be a Pharisee (Acts 23:6, Phil. 3:4–6). As a believer, Sha'ul's training as a Pharisee was filtered through his initial and subsequent revelations concerning the Messiahship of Yeshua of Nazeret.

Sha'ul's worldview was a thoroughly Jewish one, and it would have been recognized as such by his contemporaries. Jews in the Second Temple period, and especially the Pharisees, viewed themselves as living within that period of exile that Deuteronomy promised would come about because of Israel's failure to maintain covenant with God and that Daniel predicted would last not 70 years as Jeremiah prophesied, but 490 years right up to the first century C.E.

Boyarin concurs: "I would like to reclaim Paul as an important Jewish thinker. On my reading of the Pauline corpus, Paul lived and died convinced that he was a Jew living out Judaism. He represents, then, one option which Judaism could take in the first century."[10]

Alan Segal summarizes my position: "Despite the objections of a small but vocal minority, it seems certain that Paul was not only Jewish but also a Pharisee, just as he himself claims."[11]

Though Sha'ul identifies himself as a Pharisee, it impossible to know with which sect he aligned himself since Pharisaism also included subgroups led by different teachers and rabbis.

---

8 Pinchas Lapide and Peter Stuhlmacher, *Paulus: Rabbi und Apostel.*
9 Boyarin, *A Radical Jew*, 2.
10 Wright, *Paul*, 185.
11 Alan Segal, "Paul's Jewish Presuppositions," in James D. G. Dunn, *The Cambridge Companion to St. Paul*, 159.

Various competing Pharisaic sects preexisted 70 C.E. The predominate schools of thought were the Houses of Shammai and Hillel, or did Sha'ul exclusively follow the House of Gamaliel?[12]

The appearance of the resurrected Yeshua changed Sha'ul's life. His writings are replete with references to the resurrection from the dead.[13] Thus it seems to me that Sha'ul leaned toward Pharisaic Messianism, which emphasizes the resurrection from the dead. It can be defined as:

> A hope for membership in an already existent heavenly kingdom to be brought from heaven by a suddenly appearing messiah: for general judgment in which the righteous should be acquitted and the wicked condemned; for resurrection of the body and a life everlasting for the righteous; for an endless age in which God and happiness should be supreme and enjoyed forever by those whom he had justified.[14]

As Kinzer states, the *Torah*'s sacrificial system cannot impart eschatological righteousness. The answer for both Jews and Gentiles is not the *Torah* but the *euangelion* of Jesus and the *pneuma* (Spirit) he imparts.[15] That is, Sha'ul was an apocalyptic Pharisee. Bart Ehrman underscores this:

> Like many other Jews of the time—including such figures as John the Baptist and Jesus of Nazareth—Pharisees held to a kind of apocalyptic worldview that had developed toward the very end of the biblical period and down into the first century.[16]

Paul of Tarsus was born, lived and died a Jew. Raised as a Pharisee, he then joined the early Jesus movement, a first-century Jewish apocalyptic and messianic group. Paul became one of the most vocal leaders of the new movement and promoted its expansion among the Gentiles.[17]

---

12 Neusner, *In Quest*, 175–223.

13 Acts 9:1–5; 22:3–16; 26:9–18; 1 Cor. 15; Gal. 1:16; 1 Thes. 1:13–18

14 S. Mathews, "The Social Teaching of Paul. The Apocalyptic Messianism of the Pharisees," *Biblical World* 19.3.

15 Mark Kinzer, "Paul and the Torah in Apocalyptic Perspective." http://EnochSeminar.org/apocalyptic-paul-2021.

16 Bart D. Ehrman, *The Triumph of Christianity: How a Forbidden Religion Swept the World*, 44.

17 The Enoch Seminar, "Was Paul an Apocalyptic Jew? A Case in Jewish Diversity in the Second Temple Period." Conference. http://enochseminar.org/apocalyptic-paul-2021.

Who Were the Pharisees?

References to Pharisees in Literature

Though we know the Pharisees existed as a distinct group during the time of the Hasmoneans (150–140 B.C.E.), we can only gather our knowledge about them from outside sources. Neusner and Chilton emphatically state:

> How do we know anything at all about the Pharisees? No writings survive that were produced by them; all we do know is what later writers said about them. The three separate bodies of information are quite different in character. The first, Josephus (90–100 C.E.), is a systematic, coherent historical narrative. The second, the Christian contribution (65–90 C.E. for the gospels), is a well-edited collection of stories and sayings and firsthand letters. The third, the rabbinic documents of the late second through seventh century (200–600 C.E.), consists chiefly of laws, arranged by legal categories in codes and commentaries on those codes. Moreover, the purposes of the authors or compilers of the respective collections differ from one another."[18]

Neusner and Chilton add that although other writings of Judaic origin including a number of books in the Apocrypha and Pseudepigrapha of the Old Testament are attributed to Pharisaic writers, none of these documents positively identifies its author as a Pharisee.[19]

However, from these sources we can discern certain elements of Pharisaic thought as well as how they contrasted with those of the Sadducees.

Josephus

Jewish War 2:14

> Of the two schools first mentioned, the Pharisees are those who are esteemed to be the most authoritative interpreters of the Law (Torah), and count as the leading sect. They ascribe all to Fate (i.e., God's will), and yet the decision whether or not to do what is right is principally in

---

18 Neusner, *In Quest*, viii.
19 Neusner, *In Quest*, viii.

the power of men, although Fate (God's will) does take some part in every action. They say that all souls are incorruptible (immortal), but that only the souls of good men continue (after death) in another form, but that the souls of bad men are subject to eternal punishment. But the Sadducees, the second group, deny Fate (God's will) entirely, and believe that God is not concerned in our doing or not doing what is evil; and they say, that to choose to do what is good, or what is evil, is at men's own choice, and that each person must decide which he will follow. They also deny any belief in the immortality of the soul, and the punishments and rewards in Hades (i.e., after death). Moreover, the Pharisees are friendly to one another, and seek to promote concord with the general public; but the behavior of the Sadducees, even towards one another, is more disagreeable.

Antiquities of the Jews 2:4

For there was a certain sect of men that were Jews, who valued themselves highly upon the exact skill they had in the law of their fathers, and made men believe they were highly favoured by God, by whom this set of women were inveagled. These are those that are called the sect of the *Pharisees*: who were in a capacity of greatly opposing Kings. A cunning sect they were; and soon elevated to a pitch of open fighting, and doing mischief. Accordingly when all the people of the Jews gave assurance of their good will to Cæsar, and to the King's government; these very men did not swear: being above six thousand.

Antiquities 10:6

What I would now explain is this, that the Pharisees have passed down to the people a great many observances by former generations, which are not written in the laws of Moses; and for that reason the Sadducees reject those observances and say that we are to consider valid only those observances which were written (in the Torah), but are not to observe those which are derived from the tradition of our forefathers. And concerning these things great disputes and differences have arisen between the two parties. The Sadducees are able to persuade none but the rich, and have no following among the populace, while the Pharisees have the support of the masses.

Antiquities 18:1

> Now, for the Pharisees, they live simply and despise delicacies in diet. They also pay respect to their elders; and they are never so bold as to contradict them in any thing which they have proposed. Though they say that all things are determined by Fate (i.e., God's will), they do not take away freedom from men to act as they think fit. They also believe that souls are immortal, and that under the earth there will be rewards or punishments, according to whether they have lived virtuously or wickedly in this life. They are greatly influential among the townsfolk, and all Divine worship, prayers, and sacrifices are performed according to their interpretation. But the Sadducees teach that the soul dies with the body. They do not follow any observance unless it is written in the Law (Torah). Also, they think it virtuous to dispute with their teachers. But they accomplish practically nothing, however. For when they become magistrates, they have to follow the rulings of the Pharisees, otherwise the public would not tolerate them.

New Testament

The Pharisees' concern over keeping the *Torah* and the Traditions of the Elders led them to question Yeshua on numerous occasions on such subjects as fasting (Mt. 9:14) and the ritual washing of hands (Mt. 15:1–9). In turn, Yeshua chastised them for caring more about outward appearances than inner purity, focusing on tiny details (tithing on every herb) but ignoring true concerns such as justice and love of God, and their pride (Lk. 11:39–44).

Yeshua condemned the Pharisees for not practicing what they preached, but he also interacted with them socially (Lk. 7:36–50; 14:1). Though they are often seen as opponents of Yeshua, others were attracted to him, as was Nicodemus (Jn. 3:1; 7:45–53) and those who recognized he had indeed healed a blind man (9:13–38). It was Pharisees who warned Jesus about Herod's intent to kill him (Lk. 13:31), and Gamaliel, a leading Pharisee and Sha'ul's teacher, cautioned against killing Peter and the other apostles who were spreading the Gospel in Acts 5:34. In addition, Acts 15:5 indicates some of the Pharisees who were believers were among those concerned about the issue of circumcision of all believers.

Brief History of the Pharisees Origin of the Name

Shaye J. D. Cohen, in *From the Maccabees to the Mishnah*, maintains that "practically all scholars now agree that the name 'Pharisee' derives from the Hebrew and Aramaic *parush* or *perushi* (in the plural *perushim*), which means 'one who is separated,' but whether the separation is from the gentiles (as Ezra and Nehemiah speak of those who 'separated themselves from the impurity of the nations of the lands' (compare 1 Macc. 1:11), from sources of ritual impurity, or from irreligious Jews, is not as clear.... A third possibility comes from the Hebrew root *parash*, 'to interpret," as the Pharisees were noted for their expert interpretation of the biblical text.... Another suggestion is found in rabbinic sources, which equates the word *Perushim* with the word *Kedoshim*, meaning 'holy' or 'sacred.' In this interpretation, the Pharisees represent the holiest and most sacred followers of Torah."[20]

The Pharisees and the Hasmoneans

In my opinion, *Mishnat Rabbi Eliezer (Ozrov – Chancheen)*, written in the land of Israel at the close of the Roman Empire, suggests that as the defenders of *Torah* Judaism, the Pharisees considered themselves to be the spiritual descendants of Mattathias and his sons.

In his article "Did the Jewish People and Its Sages Cause the Hasmoneans to Be Forgotten?", Alon Gedalyahu conclusively demonstrates that "with the exception of the main acts perpetrated by Jannai in his conflict with the Sages, the references in rabbinic literature indicate that the Pharisaic attitude toward the Hasmoneans was quite positive."[21]

Exodus Rabbah, written in the 11th or 12th century, displays this same positive attitude:

---

20 Shaye J. D. Cohen, *From the Maccabees to the Mishnah*, 155–164.
21 Alon Gedalyahu and Israel Abrahams, "The Patriarchate of Rabban Jochanan ben Zakkai," in *Jews, Judaism and the Classical World: Studies in Jewish History in the Times of the Second Temple and Talmud.*

The four righteous men whom the Holy One blessed be He vouchsafed (to Israel) in every kingdom to save them and to spread Torah-knowledge in their midst. These are: in Babylon Daniel, Hananiah, Mishael and Azariah; in Persia Haggia, Zechariah, Malachi and Nehemiah; in the Graeco-Syrian kingdom the four sons of the Hasmonean, the eldest son, Judah, having been killed already; in Edom [i.e. the Roman Empire] Rabban Gamaliel, R. Joshua, R. Eleazar b. Azariah and R. Akiba.[22]

The Pharisees and Sadducees

The Sadducees' school of thought had also developed during the second century B.C.E. Regarding the name "Sadducees," Shaye J. D. Cohen also maintains, "Most scholars now agree that the name 'Sadducee' derives from the Hebrew word *Zeduqi* and means 'a descendant of Zadok the priest.' 'The priests of Zadok' is a regular turn of phrase in the last chapters of Ezekiel. Presumably this is a self-designation. Sadducees see themselves as descendants of Zadok the priest, that is, the true priests who are to officiate in the Temple."[23]

By the first century C.E., both the Pharisees and Sadducees were well established as the two major religious and social schools of thought. The Sadducees were more aristocratic and included the priesthood, upholding the sacrificial system. They held a very strict interpretation of the *Torah* and rejected the Oral Law. They did not believe in resurrection or an afterlife. The Pharisees embraced the Dual *Torah* (written and oral) and were concerned about keeping the minutest detail of both. They believed in angels, resurrection of the dead, and heaven. They appealed to and interacted with the "common" man and were more centered around the synagogue. The theological conflicts between the Pharisees and the Sadducees were polarizing and are well attested to in a wide range of documents including but not limited to Josephus (*Antiquities* 18:12–17) and Origen (*Book* 12:1–3).

---

22 Rabbi Avraham Blum, *Mishnat Rabbi Eliezer* (Ozrov – Chancheen), 103.
23 Shaye J. D. Cohen, *Maccabees to the Mishnah*, 159.

Pharisees and Sadducees in The New Testament

Both the Pharisees and Sadducees were vying for power and influence in the time of Yeshua. They often questioned him—not only to "trap" him (thus making him a "sinner") but also, in essence, to find out, "Whose side are you on?" One of the interesting passages in the New Testament that gives one insight into the doctrinal differences between the Pharisees and Sadducees can be found in Mark 12:18–27:

> [18] Then some *Tz'dukim* [Sadducees] came to him. They are the ones who say there is no such thing as resurrection, so they put to him a *sh'eilah*: [19] "Rabbi, Moshe wrote for us that **if a man's brother dies and leaves a wife but no child, his brother must take the wife and have children to preserve the man's family line.**[20] There were seven brothers. The first one took a wife, and when he died, he left no children. [21] Then the second one took her and died without leaving children, and the third likewise, [22] and none of the seven left children. Last of all, the woman also died. [23] In the Resurrection, whose wife will she be? For all seven had her as wife."

In response, Yeshua emphatically takes the side of the Pharisees:

> [24] Yeshua said to them, "Isn't this the reason that you go astray? because you are ignorant both of the *Tanakh* and of the power of God? [25] For when people rise from the dead, neither men nor women marry—they are like angels in heaven. [26] And as for the dead being raised, haven't you read in the book of Moshe, in the passage about the bush, how God said to him, 'I am the God of Avraham, the God of Yitz'chak and the God of Ya'akov'? [27] He is God not of the dead, but of the living! You are going far astray!"

Another example is seen when Sha'ul was brought before the Pharisees and Sadducees of the Sanhedrin for questioning, and he knowingly used their strong but conflicting beliefs about the resurrection to his advantage.

⁶ But knowing that one part of the *Sanhedrin* consisted of *Tz'dukim* [Sadducees] and the other of *P'rushim* [Pharisees], Sha'ul shouted, "Brothers, I myself am a *Parush* and the son of *P'rushim*; and it is concerning the hope of the resurrection of the dead that I am being tried!" ⁷ When he said this, an argument arose between the *P'rushim* and the *Tz'dukim*, and the crowd was divided. ⁸ For the *Tz'dukim* deny the resurrection and the existence of angels and spirits; whereas the *P'rushim* acknowledge both. ⁹ So there was a great uproar, with some of the *Torah*-teachers who were on the side of the *P'rushim* standing up and joining in—"We don't find anything wrong with this man; and if a spirit or an angel spoke to him, what of it?" (Acts 23:6–9)

Pharisees and Sadducees in Rabbinic Literature

One of the principal passages in rabbinic literature that also illustrates the contentious relationship between Pharisees and Sadducees can be found in *Yadayim* 4:6–7...

The Sadducees say, We cry out against you, O Pharisees, for you say "The Holy Scriptures render the hands unclean but the writing of Homer do not render the hands unclean."

The Sadducees say, We cry out against you, O Pharisees, for you declare pure an unbroken stream of liquid (which connects a pure vessel to an impure). The Pharisees say, We cry out against you, O Sadducees, for you declare pure a channel of water, which flows from a burial ground.

The Sadducees say, We cry out against you, O Pharisees, for you say, "If my ox or my ass have done an injury, I (the owner) am culpable, but if my bondman or bondwoman have done an injury I (the owner) am not culpable."

Also, this next passage, *Avot de Rabbi Nathan*, seems to mirror the New Testament's perception of one of the disputes between the Pharisees and Sadducees over the resurrection of the body:

Antigonus of Soko had two disciples who used to study his words. They taught them to their disciples, and their disciples to their disciples. These proceeded to examine the words closely and demanded: "Why did our ancestors see fit to say this thing? Is it possible that a laborer should do his work all day and not take his payment in the evening? If our ancestors had believed that there is another world to come and that there will be a resurrection of the dead, they would not have spoken in this manner." So they arose and split into two sects, the Sadducees and the Boethusians. The Sadducees named after the priest Zadok, and the Boethusians are named after a student Boethus. And these sectarians used silver and gold vessels all their lives. They did this (to enjoy life in this world) and not because they were ostentatious. The Sadducees said, "It is a tradition among the Pharisees to afflict themselves in this world (so as to have a greater reward in the world to come); yet in the world to come they will have nothing!"

The Growing Rabbinic Authority of the Pharisees

In the New Testament, Matthew, who portrays Yeshua as a *Torah*-observant Jew, quotes Yeshua as acknowledging the teachers of the law and the Pharisees, which are synonymous terms.

> [1] Then Yeshua addressed the crowds and his *talmidim*: [2] "The *Torah*-teachers and the *P'rushim*," he said, "sit in the seat of Moshe. [3] So whatever they tell you, take care to do it. But don't do what they do, because they talk but don't act! (Mt. 23:1–3)

Yeshua tells his followers to obey the Pharisees, the word "obey" being "an allusion to Deut. 17:9–11, the rabbis' biblical basis [proof text] for their authority to replace the priests."[24] This passage reveals the Pharisees' growing dominance over competing factions like the Sadducees.

---

24 Samuel Lachs, *A Rabbinic Commentary on The New Testament: The Gospels of Matthew, Mark, and Luke*, 366.

The Reconciliation Between Rabban Jochanan ben Zakkai and Rabban Gamaliel II

Rabban Jochanan ben Zakkai is considered to be the one who saved Judaism from complete destruction following the fall of Jerusalem and destruction of the Temple in 70 C.E. He was a student of Hillel and leader of the Pharisee party at that time. After a legendary escape from Jerusalem, he was allowed to establish a school at Jabneh, where he was joined by his followers. He was instrumental in directing the changes and transition from Temple worship to what eventually developed into Rabbinic Judaism. It would be paramount that he have the support of other leaders from the devastated Jewish and, in particular, the Pharisaic community. Gedalyahu clearly shows that many groups were antagonistic to the Patriarchate of Rabban Jochanan ben Zakkai, but that eventual reconciliation took place.

Among these groups that opposed him were the Priests (*M. Shekalim* 1:4), an array of sages including R. Nechunya b. Haqana, the teacher of R. Ishmael and Nahum of Gizmo, the teacher of R. Akiba (*T. B. Shavuot* 26a) as well as the Sons of Bathyra (*T. B. Rosh HaShanah* 29b). The tensions that existed between the supporters of Rabban Gamliel and Rabban Jochanan ben Zakkai were ameliorated by the fact that after their master's death the disciples of Rabban Jochanan ben Zakkai gave their allegiance to Rabban Gamaliel.[25]

Implicit in the subtext of *Pirkei Avot* 2:9–10 is the reconciliation that took place between the School of Rabban Jochanan ben Zakkai and the School of Rabban Gamaliel.[26]

[9] Rabban Jochanan ben Zakkai received the *Torah* from Hillel and from Shammai. He used to say: If you have learnt much *Torah* do not claim for yourself moral excellence, for to this end you were

---

25 Gedalyahu and Abrahams, "The Patriarchate."

26 For a history of the editing of the text by Rabbi Yehudah, see John Glucker, *Antiochus and the Late Academy*.

created. [10] Rabban Jochanan ben Zakkai had five disciples and these are they: Eliezer ben Hyrcanus, Joshua ben Chananiah, Yosi the Priest, Shimon ben Natanel, and Elazar ben Arach.

By declaring Rabban Jochanan ben Zakkai as receiving the *Torah* from Hillel and Shammai, this text also solidifies the authority of his teaching as well as the authority of the teaching of his five principal disciples.[27] Gamaliel II succeeded ben Zakkai and united the schools of Hillel and Shammai, further establishing the authority of the Pharisees in the development of Judaism.

I agree with Daniel Boyarin's assertion that the Pharisees created a version of rabbinic ecclesiology as a part of their attempted takeover of religious power from rival factions. I also agree with scholars such as Tzvi Zahavy that at the same time, the rabbis developed a theological system to further concretize their authority.[28]

Conclusion

Sha'ul identified himself as a Jew and as a Pharisee (Phil. 3:5), trained by Gamaliel (Acts 22:3). His revelation and acceptance of Yeshua affirmed his Pharisaic belief in the authority of the Word of God, the reality of the promised Messiah, and the surety of the resurrection of the dead and eternal life. It also led him to filter his training through the lens of his heavenly revelation, discarding the requirements of the "Traditions of the Elders" in order to present a gospel to all based on faith in Yeshua. Thus he "rethought and reworked every aspect of his native Jewish theology in light of the messiah and the spirit."[29]

---

27 Gedalyahu, "Johanan ben Zakkai." https://www.JewishVirtualLibrary.org/johanan-ben-zakkai.
28 Daniel Boyarin, *Border Lines: The Partition of Judaeo-Christianity*, 80–81.
29 Boyarin, *A Radical Jew*, 2.

FOUNDATIONAL PRINCIPLES OF RABBINIC JUDAISM

AUTHOR'S NOTE: The history and development of the foundational principles of Rabbinic Judaism is germane to one's understanding of the Letter to Titus and can be traced through a wide range of Jewish and non-Jewish texts beginning with the *Tanakh* and concluding with the final editing in 500 C.E. of the *Babylonian Talmud*. The purpose of this essay is to examine and analyze the key foundational principles of Rabbinic Judaism, namely the concept of the Dual *Torah* and the concept of rabbinic authority.

The Concept of the Dual *Torah*

Rabbinic Judaism transformed Judaism from a single-*Torah* system into a dual-*Torah* system. "In the Judaism of the dual *Torah*, the rabbis asserted that Moses received a twofold revelation on Sinai. The *Pentateuch* was one part of that corpus, the written law. The second part was the oral law. The doctrine of revelation encompassed in the rabbinic assertion of a dual *Torah* is complex, elastic, and fraught with deliberate ambiguity. Its promulgators suggested that the oral law remained abstract, transmitted from teacher to student, until given a sanctioned written form in the teachings of rabbis."[30] In other words, the "*Mikra* (Scripture), *Mishna*, *Talmud* and *Aggada*, even what an advanced student will teach before his master was already said to Moses on Sinai."[31] The concept of the dual *Torah* system, which is at the same time the Rabbis' version of their ecclesiastical history, is explicitly stated in *B. T. Megilah* 19b:

> R. Hiyya b. Abba also said in the name of R. Johanan: What is the meaning of the verse, And on them was written according to all the words which the Lord spoke with you in the mount? It teaches us

---

30 Tzvee Zahavy, "It Is Not in Heaven: Judaic Systems, Laws and Discordant Discourses."
  https://www.tzvee.com/Home/it-is-not-in-heaven.
31 Shmuel Safrai, *The Literature of the Sages, First Part: Oral Tora, Halakha, Mishna, Tosefta, Talmud, External Tractates*, 57.

that the Holy One, blessed be He, showed Moses the minutiae of the *Torah*, and the minutiae of the Scribes, and the innovations, which would be introduced by the Scribes; and what are these?

The Concept of Rabbinic Authority

The second concept that is explicit in the teaching and the writings of the Sages is that the rabbis are the sole legitimate interpreters of the *Torah* and *halakhic* disputes. That is, the meaning of the *Torah* could only be brought out through "the concentrated and devoted involvement of the Sages and their students with Moses' *Torah*."[32] *Baba Metziah* 59:3b–4 is a prime example of this concept and cites a portion of Deuteronomy 30:12, "The *Torah* is not in Heaven," as a proof text to support the rabbis' contention.

> [3b] Again he said to them: "If the *Halakhah* agrees with me, let it be proved from Heaven!" Whereupon a Heavenly Voice cried out: "Why do ye dispute with R. Eliezer, seeing that in all matters the *Halakhah* agrees with him!" But R. Joshua arose and exclaimed: "It is not in heaven." [4] What did he mean by this?—Said R. Jeremiah: That the *Torah* had already been given at Mount Sinai; we pay no attention to a Heavenly Voice, because Thou has long since written in the *Torah* at Mount Sinai, after the majority must one incline. (*Baba Metziah* 59:3b–4)

The *Gemara* goes on to explain the meaning of the phrase "It is not in Heaven":

> Rabbi Yirmeyah said in reply: Since God already gave the *Torah* to the Jewish people on Mount Sinai, we no longer pay attention to heavenly voices that attempt to intervene in matters of *Halakhah*. For You, God, already wrote in the *Torah* at Mount Sinai (Exodus 23:2), "After the majority to incline." From this verse we learn that *halakhic* disputes must be resolved by majority vote of the Rabbis. God could not contradict His own decision to allow *Torah* questions to be decided by free debate and majority vote.[33]

---

32 Adin Steinsaltz, *The Talmud: The Steinsaltz Edition*, 237.
33 Steinsaltz, *The Talmud*, 237.

For the rabbis, miracles and the Heavenly Voice are not considered authoritative in deciding matters of *halakhah*. They believe the *Torah* itself recognizes only the outstanding *Torah* scholars of each generation as the authoritative interpreters of the law, hence the *Gemara*'s statement that the *Torah* is "not in heaven."[34]

The above citation from *Baba Metziah* is representative of other statements found in rabbinic literature that seek to legitimize the authority of the rabbis and delegitimize competing claims by other individuals and groups to authoritatively interpret the *Torah* and make binding *halakhic* decisions. In other words, as Tzvee Zahavy so aptly puts it:

> The rabbinic holy men of the late antique era claimed the sole authority to author and interpret the law for their communities. They openly asserted the strict limitations of divine power. They thereby entrenched their prestige firmly as masters of discursive analysis, denying it to rival claimants such as those who based their stature on mystical revelation or other forms of charismatic expertise or feats.[35]

The Men of the *Knesset HaGedolah* – The Great Assembly

In *Pirkei Avot*, the rabbis claimed their spiritual genealogy included "the men of the Great Assembly" (*Avot* 1:1). The *Knesset Ha-Gedolah* ("Great Assembly" or "Great Synagogue") was a legislative body of 120 members, composed of prophets, scribes, sages and teachers. According to tradition, it was originated by Ezra the scribe upon his return from the Babylonian captivity (*Megillah* 17b).[36] The following passages portray Ezra as the prototypical rabbi / patriarch / *nassi* on which the rabbis based their model:

> [1] While Ezra was praying and making confession, weeping, and prostrated before the house of God, a huge crowd of Isra'el's men, women and children gathered around him; and the people were

---

34 Steinsaltz, *The Talmud*, 237.
35 Zahavy, "It Is Not in Heaven."
36 Hyman E. Goldin, *Ethics of the Fathers*, 3.

weeping bitterly. ² Sh'khanyah the son of Yechi'el, one of the descendants of 'Eilam, spoke up and said to 'Ezra, "We have acted treacherously toward our God by marrying foreign women from the peoples of the land. But despite this, there is still hope for Isra'el.

³ We should make a covenant with our God to send away all these wives, along with their children, in obedience to the advice of *Adonai* and of those who tremble at the *mitzvah* of our God; let us act in accordance with the *Torah.* ⁴ Stand up, and do your duty, for we are with you; take courage, and do it!"

⁵ 'Ezra stood up, and he made the chief *cohanim*, the *L'vi'im* and all Isra'el swear that they would act according to what had been said; and they took the oath. ⁶ 'Ezra then left his place in front of the house of God and went to the room of Y'hochanan the son of Elyashiv. After going there, he neither ate food nor drank water; because he was mourning over the treachery of the exiles.

⁷ A proclamation was issued throughout Y'hudah and Yerushalayim that all the exiles were to assemble in Yerushalayim; ⁸ and that whoever didn't come within three days, in answer to the summons from the officials and leaders, would forfeit all he owned and himself be banished from the community of the exiles. ⁹ All the men of Y'hudah and Binyamin assembled in Yerushalayim within the three days. It was the twentieth day of the ninth month. All the people sat in the open place in front of the house of God, trembling because of this matter and because of the heavy rain. ¹⁰ 'Ezra the *cohen* stood up and addressed them: "You have acted treacherously by marrying foreign women and have thus increased Isra'el's guilt. ¹¹ Now, therefore, make confession to *ADONAI*, the God of your ancestors; and do what will please him by separating yourselves from the peoples of the land and from the foreign women." ¹² In response, the whole assembly cried aloud, "Yes, our duty is to do as you have said.

¹³ But there are many people, and it's the rainy season — we can't stay out here in the open. Also, it isn't the work of a day or two; for there are many of us who have committed this crime. ¹⁴ Let our leaders represent the whole community; and let all those in our cities who have married foreign women appear at prearranged times, accompanied by the elders and judges of each city; until our God's

fierce anger over this has been turned away from us." [15] Only Yonatan the son of 'Asah'el and Yachz'yah the son of Tikvah, supported by Meshulam and Shabtai the *Levi*, opposed this.

[16] The exiles did as agreed. 'Ezra the *cohen* chose heads of fathers' clans by name, and they began their sessions to look into the matter on the first day of the tenth month. [17] They finished dealing with all the men who had married foreign women by the first day of the first month. (Ezra 10:1–17)

These passages demonstrate that though Ezra was a *Kohen*, he also functioned as the chief rabbi of the Jewish community in Jerusalem and Judah. His *halakhic* decision regarding the divorcing of foreign wives was not only accepted by the priests, leaders and residents of Jerusalem, but it was also accepted by all the men in the outlying regions of Judah (cf. Ezra 10:14).

Though not stated in these passages, I contend that the rabbis derived the idea of a "spiritual genealogy" from Ezra 7:1–6. As a direct descendant of Aaron, his genealogy establishes him with the credentials and authority to interpret the *Torah* and to make *halakhic* decisions (cf. *B.T. Sanhedrin* 21b). Claiming to be a part of his genealogy would give them the same authority.

[1] After these events, during the reign of Artach'shashta king of Persia, 'Ezra the son of S'rayah, the son of 'Azaryah, the son of Hilkiyah, [2] the son of Shalum, the son of Tzadok, the son of Achituv, [3] the son of Amaryah, the son of 'Azaryah, the son of M'rayot, [4] the son of Z'rachyah, the son of 'Uzi, the son of Buki, [5] the son of Avishua, the son of Pinchas, the son of Eli'ezer, the son of Aharon the *cohen hagadol*—[6] this 'Ezra went up from Bavel. He was a scribe, expert in the *Torah* of Moshe, which ADONAI the God of Isra'el had given; and the king granted him everything he asked for, since the hand of ADONAI his God was on him.

By examining the above-cited texts, we have been able to trace the rabbis' version of their ecclesiastical history as well as the development of their key theological principles, those being the concept of the Dual *Torah* and the concept of Rabbinic Authority.

RABBIS AND THEIR *TALMIDIM*

Sha'ul implicitly understood that his role as an apostle was to make *talmidim* of all nations—*talmidim* who were trained and given the authority to speak on behalf of the Kingdom of God (Mt. 28:19; cf. *Pirkei Avot* 1:1). This is a relationship and process that Sha'ul personally understood because he was the *talmid* of Rav Gamli'el.

> I am a Jew, born in Tarsus of Cilicia, but brought up in this city and trained at the feet of Gamli'el in every detail of the *Torah* of our forefathers. I was a zealot for God, as all of you are today. (Acts 22:3)

In Judaism, teachers are frequently portrayed as father figures; thus, when Sha'ul addresses Titus as "my son," he is, by common practice, identifying Titus as his *talmid*. The Stone Edition Chumash's explanation of Numbers 3:1–3 gives one insight into the basis for this concept:

> [1] *(iv)* These are the descendants of Aharon and Moshe as of the day when *ADONAI* spoke with Moshe on Mount Sinai. [2] The names of the sons of Aharon are: Nadav the firstborn, Avihu, El'azar and Itamar. [3] These were the names of the sons of Aharon the *cohen*, whom he anointed and ordained as *cohanim*. (Numbers 3:1–3)

> The *Talmud* (*Sanhedrin* 19b) wonders why this passage names only the sons of Aaron but calls them the offspring of Aaron and Moses. From this description, the Talmud infers that the one who teaches *Torah* to someone else's children is regarded as if he had begotten them. Because he taught the *Torah* to Aaron's four sons, Moses became their spiritual father, just as Aaron was their biological father. (Rashi; Ramban)[37]

Reinhold Neudecker writes: "The rabbinic interpretation of biblical 'father' and 'son' as 'master' and 'disciple' is common."[38] And according to Boyarin, "becoming a 'disciple of the sages' often meant accepting a rabbinic father in place of one's biological father."[39]

---

37 Nosson Scherman, *The Chumash: The Torah, Haftaros and Five Megillos with a Commentary Anthologized from the Rabbinic Writings*, 737.
38 Reinhard Neudecker, "Master-Disciple/Disciple-Master Relationship in Rabbinic Judaism and in the Gospels," *Gregorianum* 80.2, 245–261.
39 Daniel Boyarin, *The Talmud – A Personal Take: Selected Essays,* 83.

The *Sefer Madda* (*Book of Knowledge, Talmud Torah*) exemplifies the idea that becoming a "disciple of the Sages" often meant not only accepting a rabbinic father in place of one's biological father but that the role of a rabbi could even supersede that of a father.

> Just as a person is commanded to honor his father and hold him in awe, so, too, is he obligated to honor his teacher and hold him in awe.
>
> [Indeed, the measure of honor and awe] due one's teacher exceeds that due one's father. His father brings him into the life of this world, while his teacher, who teaches him wisdom, brings him into the life of the world to come.
>
> [Accordingly], if he saw a lost object belonging to his father and one belonging to his teacher, the lost object belonging to his teacher takes precedence. If his father and his teacher are both carrying loads, he should relieve his teacher's load, and then his father's. If his father and his teacher are held as captives, he should redeem his teacher, and afterwards, redeem his father." (*Talmud Torah* 5:1)[40]

This section of *Talmud Torah* concludes with the following summary statement:

> There is no greater honor than that due a teacher, and no greater awe than that due a teacher. Our Sages declared: "Your fear of your teacher should be equivalent to your fear of Heaven."[41]

Samuel Lachs connects these statements in *Talmud Torah* 5:1 with Luke 14:26, which, in a similar fashion, declares that a *talmid's* rabbi is to be more highly esteemed than one's father.[42]

> If anyone comes to me and does not hate his father, his mother, his wife, his children, his brothers and his sisters, yes, and his own life besides, he cannot be my *talmid*. (Lk 14:26)

---

40 https://www.Chabad.org/library/article_cdo/aid/904958/jewish/Sefer-Madda.htm.
41 Sefer Madda.
42 Lachs, *Rabbinic Commentary*, 187.

Once the relationship of rabbi (father) and *talmid* (son) is established, the *talmid* would be committed to following his rabbi. Most scholars agree that the model for the rabbi-*talmid* relationship is based on the paradigm of Elijah and Elisha.

> [19] So he [Elijah] left and found Elisha the son of Shafat. He was plowing with twelve yoke of oxen; he himself was behind the twelfth. Eliyahu went over to him and threw his cloak on him. [20] He left the oxen, ran after Eliyahu and said, "Please let me kiss my father and mother good-bye; then **I will follow you**." He answered, "Go; but return, because of what I did to you." [21] Elisha stopped following him. Then he took the yoke of oxen, slaughtered them, cooked their meat over the wooden yokes of the oxen and gave it to the people to eat. Then he got up, went after Eliyahu and became his servant. (1 Kings 19:19–21)

The phrase "I will follow you" is a Semitic term understood to mean "become your disciple,"[43] and it is frequently associated with becoming Yeshua's disciple.

> "Come, after [follow] me," Jesus said, "and I will send you out to fish for people." (Mt. 4:19)

> Immediately Jesus called to them; and they left their father Zebedee in the boat with the hired workers, and went away to **follow** Him [becoming His disciples, believing and trusting in Him and following His example]. (Mark 1:20, *The Amplified Bible*)[44]

> [18] One of the leaders asked him, "Good rabbi, what should I do to obtain eternal life?" [19] Yeshua said to him, "Why are you calling me good? No one is good but God! [20] You know the *mitzvot*—'Don't commit adultery, don't murder, don't steal, don't give false testimony, honor your father and mother...'" [21] He replied, "I have kept all these since I was a boy." [22] On hearing this Yeshua said to him, "There is one thing you still lack. Sell whatever you have, distribute the proceeds to the poor, and you will have riches in heaven. Then come, **follow** me!" (Lk. 18:18–22)

---

43 Lachs, *Rabbinic Commentary*, 17.
44 *The Amplified Bible*.

Titus, as a *talmid*, would thus accompany Sha'ul on his comings and goings, as evidenced here:

> As for Titus, he is my partner who works with me on your behalf; and the other brothers with him are emissaries of the congregations and bring honor to the Messiah. (2 Corinthians 8:23)

> Then after fourteen years I again went up to Yerushalayim, this time with Bar-Nabba; and I took with me Titus. (Gal. 2:1)

On a humorous note, the *Talmud* (*B. Berakhot* 62a) presents a comical example of a disciple who followed his rabbi too closely:

> It was taught in a *baraita* in tractate *Derekh Eretz* that Rabbi Akiva said: I once entered the bathroom after my teacher Rabbi Yehoshua, and I learned three things from observing his behavior: I learned that one should not defecate while facing east and west, but rather while facing north and south; I learned that one should not uncover himself while standing, but while sitting, in the interest of modesty; and I learned that one should not wipe with his right hand, but with his left. Ben Azzai, a student of Rabbi Akiva, said to him: You were impertinent to your teacher to that extent that you observed that much? He replied: It is *Torah*, and I must learn.[45]

To "follow" a rabbi as his *talmid* also carries with it a commitment to become his rabbi's servant. Neudecker emphasizes the importance of a *talmid* (disciple) serving his master:

> One of the most important avenues leading to the learning of *Torah* is "serving" the master. For this reason, discipleship was frequently called "service to the Sages" (*Av* 6:6). Concretely this meant that the disciple was expected to spend a portion of his time engaged in menial labor for his master. According to a third-century authority, this was work that was normally assigned to a slave. To distinguish the role of the disciple from the role of the slave, a ruling dictated that a disciple should not loosen his master's sandals in public lest it would be thought that he was really a slave (*bKet* 96a).[46]

---

45 "Berakhot 62a." https://www.Sefaria.org/Berakhot.62a.
46 Neudecker, "Master-Disciple," 255.

Notice the parallel idea regarding the loosening of the sandals as expressed by John the Baptist:

> [7] He [John] proclaimed: "After me is coming someone who is more powerful than I—I'm not worthy even to bend down and untie his sandals. (Mark 1:7)

According to the writings of the sages, a *talmid* would live near or with his rabbi so he could observe his master's lifestyle to learn how to apply and incorporate the principles of the *Torah* for daily living. Yeshua instructed those who followed him:

> "**Come** to me, all of you who are struggling and burdened, and I will give you rest. [29] Take my yoke upon you **and learn from me**, because I am gentle and humble in heart, and you will find rest for your souls. (Mt. 11:28–29)

Then he opened their minds, so that they could understand the *Tanakh*…. (Lk. 24:45)

The master and his *talmid* would study the Written *Torah* (Hebrew: תורה שבכתב, *Torah she-bi-khtav*), which included the written five Books of Moses, as well as the or Oral Law (Hebrew: תורה שבעל פה, *Torah she-be-ʿal peh*, lit. "*Torah* that is on the mouth"), which represents those laws, statutes and legal interpretations that were not recorded in the Written *Torah*. It was very important for Titus to know and understand the Oral *Torah* and the writings of the Sages as well as the Scriptures themselves so he was equipped to deal with the issues raised by the members of the Circumcision Party. Sha'ul's tutelage and guidance would have prepared Titus in all areas.

By being cognizant of the teacher/*talmid* relationship between Sha'ul and Titus, we can more fully understand the extensiveness of Titus' training and Sha'ul's confidence in his *talmid*. By addressing Titus as "my son," Sha'ul is confirming that Titus has been personally and formally trained as his rabbinic disciple, and is well-equipped to be his apostolic delegate to Crete.

A BRIEF HISTORY OF THE SYNAGOGUE

Tell the whole **community** (*edah*) of Israel that on the tenth day of this month each man is to take a lamb for his family, one for each household. (Ex 12:3, NIV)

These are the commandments the Lord proclaimed in a loud voice to your whole **assembly** (*qahal*) there on the mountain from out of the fire... (Deut 5:22a)

[28] Even so, *ADONAI* my God, pay attention to your servant's prayer and plea, listen to the cry and prayer that your servant is praying before you today, [29] that your eyes will be open toward this **house** night and day—toward the place concerning which you said, 'My name will be there'—to listen to the prayer your servant will pray toward this place. [30] Yes, listen to the plea of your servant, and also that of your people Isra'el when they pray toward this place. Hear in heaven where you live; and when you hear, forgive! (1 Kgs. 8:28–30)

[Her husband] asked, "Why are you going to him today? It isn't *Rosh-Hodesh* and it isn't *Shabbat*." She said, "It's all right. ... So she set out and came to the man of God at Mount Carmel (2 Kgs. 4:23, 25)

The word "synagogue" comes from the Greek *synagōgē*, the Hebrew equivalent being *edah* ("community, congregation"; Ex. 12:3) or *qahal* ("assembly"; Deut. 5:22). Possible references to communal religious gatherings that may have functioned as the precursors of the synagogue include Solomon's prayer at the dedication of the Temple as a place of prayer. The existence of specific places of public prayer and ritual observance may also be evidenced in the account of the Shunamite woman's knowing where to find Elisha upon the death of her son. In the *Tanakh*, King Hezikiah's reading of the covenant is a further example of the public reading of the *Torah*:

[1] Then the king summoned all the leaders of Y'hudah and Yerushalayim, and they assembled with him. [2] The king went up to the house of *Adonai* with all the men of Y'hudah, all those living in Yerushalayim, the *cohanim*, the prophets and all the people, both small and great; and he read in their hearing everything written in the scroll of the covenant that had been found in the house of *ADONAI*. [3] The king stood on the platform and made a covenant in the presence

of *ADONAI* to live following *ADONAI*, observing his *mitzvot*, instructions and regulations wholeheartedly and with all his being, to confirm the words of the covenant written in this scroll. All the people stood, pledging themselves to keep the covenant. (2 Kgs. 23:1–3)

Philo (*Life of Moses* 3.27), Josephus (*Antiquities* 16.6.2), and Acts (14:1; 17:1–2; 18:4, 7) attest to the presence of places of prayer (i.e., synagogues) throughout the Mediterranean world, from Italy eastward to Greece, Asia Minor, as well as Egypt and North Africa.[47]

The earliest-known place of prayer as a religious institution first appears in the Diaspora. Literary material indicates "places of prayer" existed in Egypt as early as 250 B.C.E.[48] The term *proseuche* was widely used in the Diaspora and is attested to before the use of the more-common term "synagogue."

The earliest-known Judaean synagogue (first century B.C.E. or C.E.) was a building erected in Jerusalem.[49] Theodotus mentions the activities of this synagogue as the reading of the *Torah*, observance of religious precepts, and hospitality for visitors.[50]

The synagogues in the Diaspora and Judea each developed their own traditions (*minhag*) to meet the demands of their local situations. Lee I. Levine, in his work *The Nature and Origin of the Palestinian Synagogue Reconsidered*, states:

Given this wide-ranging diversity among first-century synagogues, what, then, was the common denominator among them? What characteristics or functions were regarded as basic? The answer is that, first and foremost, the synagogue served the full range of needs of a particular community. As documented in contemporary sources, such functions included political meetings, social gatherings, courts, schools, hostels, charity activities, slave manumission, meals (sacred or otherwise), and, of course, religious-liturgical functions.[51]

---

47 Levine and Brettler, *Jewish Annotated New Testament*, 520.
48 Bloch, *The Biblical and Historical Background of the Jewish Holy Days*, 16.
49 Cohen, "Temple and the Synagogue."
50 Stefan C. Reif, *Judaism and Hebrew Prayer: New Perspectives on Jewish Liturgical History*.
51 Lee I. Levine, "The Nature and Origin of the Palestinian Synagogue Reconsidered," in *Journal of Biblical Literature* 115.3.

Shaye J. D. Cohen adds:

> Ancient synagogues also served as assembly halls or community centres, much as the Temple itself often did. Hence the synagogue is an amalgamation of three separate institutions: a prayer-house, a study-hall or school, and a community centre. The time and pace at which this amalgamation was affected are as unknown as are the origins of each of the institutions which comprise the whole.[52]

Over a period, of time, the synagogue was also known as *Beit Knesset* ("place of assembly").

TORAH CONTROVERSIES

> And no longer pay attention to Judaistic myths or to the commands of people who reject the truth. (Titus 1:14)

> But avoid stupid controversies, genealogies, quarrels and fights about the *Torah*; because they are worthless and futile. (Titus 3:9)

What these "Judaistic myths," "commands of people," "stupid controversies," "genealogies" and "quarrels about the *Torah*" referred to in Titus were actually addressing has been debated and speculated upon throughout church history. Theories abound!

Samuel Sandmel writes in *Myths, Genealogies, and Jewish Myths and the Writing of Gospels* that many first-century Jews enjoyed "devotional" works full of inventive stories about people in the genealogies of the Old Testament.[53] Hort, in his important book *Judaistic Christianity*, posits that the stories reflect Jewish interests in legendary ancestor stories.[54] Ceslas Spicq, in *Saint Paul: Les Épîtres Pastorales*, clearly demonstrates he agrees with Hort and Sandmel.[55]

---

52 Cohen, "Temple and the Synagogue."

53 Samuel Sandmel, "Myths, Genealogies, and Jewish Myths and the Writing of Gospels," in *Hebrew Union College Annual* 27. https://www.jstor.org/stable/i23502593.

54 Hort, *Judaistic Christianity.*

55 Ceslas Spicq, *Saint Paul: Les Épîtres Pastorales*, 21.

R. H. Charles identifies the *Book of Jubilees* as an example of this type of non-canonical writing that was popular with the sect that produced the Dead Sea Scrolls. *Jubilees* retells the events from creation to the giving of the Law, incorporating fanciful legends about the patriarchs and "expanding upon" the ancestry lists in Genesis.[56] Following is an example of a legendary ancestor story about Abraham (Abram), taken from *Book of Jubilees* 11:13–21.

> And in this thirty-ninth jubilee, in the second week in the first year, [1870 A.M.] Terah took to himself a wife, and her name was 'Edna, the daughter of 'Abram, the daughter of his father's sister. And in the seventh year of this week [1876 A.M.] she bare him a son, and he called his name **Abram**, by the name of the father of his mother; for he had died before his daughter had conceived a son.

> **And the child** began to understand the errors of the earth that all went astray after graven images and after uncleanness, and his father taught him writing, and he was two weeks of years old, [1890 A.M.] and he separated himself from his father, that he might not worship idols with him.

> **And he** began to pray to the Creator of all things that He might save him from the errors of the children of men, and that his portion should not fall into error after uncleanness and vileness.

> And the seed time came for the sowing of seed upon the land, and they all went forth together to protect their seed against the ravens, and **Abram** went forth with those that went, and the child was a lad of fourteen years.

> And a cloud of ravens came to devour the seed, and **Abram** ran to meet them before they settled on the ground and cried to them before they settled on the ground to devour the seed, and said, 'Descend not: return to the place whence ye came,' and they proceeded to turn back.

---

56 Robert Henry Charles, *The Apocrypha and Pseudepigrapha of the Old Testament in English*.

> **And he** caused the clouds of ravens to turn back that day seventy times, and of all the ravens throughout all the land where Abram was there settled there not so much as one. And all who were with **him** throughout all the land saw him cry out, and all the ravens turn back, and his name became great in all the land of the Chaldees.
>
> And there came to him this year all those that wished to sow, and **he** went with them until the time of sowing ceased: and they sowed their land, and that year they brought enough grain home and eat and were satisfied.[57]

R. C. Sproul, in one of his messages, comments on a parallel passage in 1 Timothy that the "myths and endless genealogies" are probably evidence that "Jewish legends [such as those in *Jubilees*] were a part of the errors taught in the church there."[58]

Amy Jill-Levine and Marc Zvi Brettler in their book *The Jewish Annotated New Testament* posit that in addition to the Jewish myths referring to ancestor stories that they may be referring to the genealogies of Yeshua.

> The letter [Letter to Titus] closes by adding "genealogies" and "quarrels about the law" to the list of disagreeable beliefs and behaviors (3:9). These genealogies may be the generational lists that appear in the Jewish Scriptures (Gen. 10; 11, 10–32; 1 Chr. 1–9), and the speculations about them may be similar to those found among the Dead Sea Scrolls (1QapGen). Alternatively, the genealogies may be of Jesus himself, of which two conflicting ones are extant (Mt. 1 and Lk. 3)[59]

Other commentators, such as A. T. Hanson[60] and Andreas J. Köstenberger, believe the phrase "Jewish myths" refers to writings that reflect the doctrines of Jewish Gnosticism. According to Köstenberger,

---

57 Charles, *Apocrypha and Pseudepigrapha.*
58 "A Solemn Charge: Reformed Bible Studies & Devotionals."
 www.ligonier.org/learn/devotionals/solemn-charge.
59 Levine and Brettler, *Jewish Annotated New Testament*, 401.
60 Anthony Tyrrell Hanson, *The Pastoral Epistles: Based on the Revised Standard Version*, 57.

"Jewish myths" were apparently ascetic, an amalgam of Jewish food laws and a dualistic rejection of the material realm (cf. Col. 2:21–22).[61]

Unfortunately, not knowing what "Jewish myths" and similar phrases were addressing has historically led to the church tendency to delete all "Jewish-ness" from the assembly. Samuel Krauss comments:

> This passage from Titus concerning Jewish fables is cited on numerous occasions by the church fathers. The church fathers were extremely negative towards the Jewish interpretation of Scripture. The writings of Eusebius are representative of their negative attitude. His work, *Demononstratio Evangelica*, was avowedly written as a direct attack on the Jews. He holds that, in their exposition of Scripture, the Jews are guilty of serious errors, and efforts should be made to induce them to abandon their heresies; that is to say, religious disputations should be encouraged with the view of persuading them to give up their faith.[62]

> Regardless of what ideas or cultural issues these phrases were specifically referring to, Sha'ul clearly warns Titus that they have no place in the Messianic community. Marc Hirshman from the Hebrew University of Jerusalem advocates: "In the pastoral letter to Titus, Paul is said to have warned the Cretans from heeding 'Jewish myths and human commandments' (Titus 1:14). It would seem that the author is warning the audience against the Jewish misunderstanding of Scripture on two fronts, *aggadah* and *halakhah*, interpretation and observance."[63]

In my opinion, the phrase "Jewish myths" is also related to the concept of the "Tradition of the Elders," which Yeshua addressed on numerous occasions.

> [1] Then some *P'rushim* and *Torah*-teachers from Yerushalayim came to Yeshua and asked him, [2] "Why is it that your *talmidim* break the Tradition of the Elders?" (Mt. 15:1–2; cf. Mk. 7:1–3)

---

61 Köstenberger, *Commentary on 1–2 Timothy and Titus.*
62 Samuel Krauss, *The Jews in the Works of the Church Fathers: Sources for Understanding the Agaddah,* 82.
63 Hirshman, "Origen's View."

Samuel Tobias Lachs presents a cogent definition of the phrase "Tradition of the Elders":

> This expression goes back to *divre zeqenim* or *mizvot zeqenim*, "the words of the elders" or "the commandments of the elders," or even perhaps to *divre soferim*, "the words of the scribes," and these terms are always used to differentiate these teachings, part of the Oral Law, and the commands of the *Torah*, which are the Written Law. [Cf., e.g., Tj Ber. 1,3b(47); B. Er. 13a; 21b; Tan. Naso, 29] *Tradition* Gr. *paradosis* could also go back to Heb. *mesoret*, since the verb m-s-r means "to hand over." [Cf. Josephus, ANT. XIII.29.7; M. Avot 1:1][64]

Yeshua points out that the Word of God was being nullified for the sake of man-made traditions:

> [5] The *P'rushim* and the *Torah*-teachers asked him, "Why don't your *talmidim* live in accordance with the Tradition of the Elders, but instead eat with ritually unclean hands?" [6] Yeshua answered them, "Yesha'yahu was right when he prophesied about you hypocrites— as it is written,
>
> > 'These people honor me with their lips,
> > but their hearts are far away from me.
> > [7] Their worship of me is useless,
> > because they teach man-made rules as if they were doctrines.'
>
> [8] "You depart from God's command and hold onto human tradition. [9] Indeed," he said to them, "you have made a fine art of departing from God's command in order to keep your tradition!" (Mk. 7:5–9)

Though the exact meaning of the phrase "Judaistic myths" is debated, the point is that relying on extra-biblical sources to interpret the Scriptures leads to foolish arguments that nullify the Word of God and, in turn, eventually end up in the rejection of the truth of the Good News. Traditions, the writings of the Sages, commentaries, lexicons, et

---

64 Lachs, *Rabbinic Commentary*, 245.

al., can be valuable tools to gain insight into the significance of biblical culture, history and language, but they are no substitute for the Bible and pale in comparison to it.

Because of his training and relationship with Sha'ul, Titus is commissioned and equipped to combat these controversies and help the community of believers build their faith on God's Word.

> As it is written, "All *Scripture* [not *traditions*, et al.] is God-breathed and is valuable for teaching the truth, convicting of sin, correcting faults and training in right living. (1 Tim. 3:16)

MESORAH

The idea behind a careful chain of oral transmission of Jewish religious truth and/or tradition finds its parallel in the Rabbinic concept of *Mesorah*. Theologically, Orthodox Jews believe Moshe (Moses) received the *Torah* and each of its commandments (*mitzvos*) as well as their oral commentary from G-d. The oral traditions include not only the correct interpretation of the *Torah* but also the acceptable principles for leading a godly life. Tremendous care was taken to ensure that even the smallest detail was transmitted correctly.[65] This foundational belief is clearly delineated in the first *Mishnah* in *Pirkei Avot*.

> Moshe Rabbeinu received the *Torah* from Har Sinai and transmitted it to Yehoshua, and Yehoshua to the Elders, and the Elders to the Prophets, and the Prophets transmitted it to the Men of the Great Assembly.[66]

Several verses in the *Brit Chadashah* indicate Sha'ul affirmed the practice of *Mesorah*, meaning he transmitted to his *talmidim* that which the Lord revealed to him exclusive of the oral Traditions of the Elders.

Regarding sound teaching:

> But thank God that although you used to be slaves of sin, you gave wholehearted obedience to the teaching that was **handed down to you**, which provides a pattern. (Rom. 6:17, CEB)

Regarding the Lord's Passover meal:

> For what **I received** from the Lord is just what **I passed on to you**— that the Lord Yeshua, on the night he was betrayed, took bread… (1 Cor. 11:23)

---

65 For a more detailed explanation regarding the concept of *Mesorah*, see "Mesorah: The Chain of Tradition." https://Torah.org/learning/basics-primer-torah-mesora.

66 Avot 1:1 מֹשֶׁה קִבֵּל תּוֹרָה מִסִּינַי, וּמְסָרָהּ לִיהוֹשֻׁעַ, וִיהוֹשֻׁעַ לִזְקֵנִים, וּזְקֵנִים לִנְבִיאִים, וּנְבִיאִים מְסָרוּהָ לְאַנְשֵׁי כְנֶסֶת הַגְּדוֹלָה

Regarding the Good News:

> [3] For among the first things **I passed on to you** was what **I also received**, namely this: the Messiah died for our sins, in **accordance with what the *Tanakh* says**; [4] and he was buried; and he was raised on the third day, in accordance with what the *Tanakh* says... (1 Cor. 15:3–4)

Notice the sequence in 1 Corinthians 15:3–4. Yeshua transmitted the Good News to Sha'ul, which he transmitted to the Corinthians, which Sha'ul emphasizes was based on Scripture. Sha'ul's implementation of the principle of *Mesorah* in his letters represents his training as a Pharisee.

BIBLIOGRAPHY

Abrahams, Israel. *Studies in Pharisaism and the Gospels*. Cambridge: University Press, 1917.

Gedalyahu, Alon, and Israel Abrahams. *Jews, Judaism and the Classical World: Studies in Jewish History in the Times of the Second Temple and Talmud*. Skokie, IL: Varda Books, 2012.

Bass, Chris. "Were Titus and Luke Brothers?" February 25, 2019. https://PastorChrisBass.wordpress.com/2017/10/09/were-titus-and-luke-brothers.

Ben Maimon, Rabbi Moshe. *Sefer Madda – The Book of Knowledge*. Trans. Eliyahu Touger. https://www.chabad.org/library/article_cdo/aid/904958/jewish/Sefer-Madda.htm.

Bloch, Abraham P. *The Biblical and Historical Background of the Jewish Holy Days*. New York: KTAV, 1978.

Boyarin, Daniel. *Border Lines the Partition of Judaeo-Christianity*. Philadelphia: University of Pennsylvania Press, 2007.

Boyarin, Daniel. *Dying for God: Martyrdom and the Making of Christianity and Judaism*. Stanford, CA: Stanford University Press, 2007.

Boyarin, Daniel. *The Talmud – A Personal Take: Selected Essays*. Tübingen: Mohr Siebeck, 2017.

Bruce, F. F. *Paul: The Apostle of the Heart Set Free*. Grand Rapids: Eerdmans, 1998.

Campbell, Mike. "Titus." *Behind the Name*. https://www.BehindTheName.com/name/titus.

Charles, R. H. *The Apocrypha and Pseudepigrapha of the Old Testament in English: With Introductions and Critical and Explanatory Notes to the Several Books*. Oxford: Clarendon Press, 1913.

Chilton, Bruce David, and Jacob Neusner. *Classical Christianity and Rabbinic Judaism Comparing Theologies*. Grand Rapids: Baker Academic, 2004.

Clark, Matityahu. *Etymological Dictionary of Biblical Hebrew: Based on the Commentaries of Rabbi Samson Raphael Hirsch*. New York: Feldheim Publishers, 2000.

Clements, R. E., Matthew Black, and A. T. Hanson. *New Century Bible Commentary: The Pastoral Epistles*. Grand Rapids: Eerdmans, 1981.

Cohen, Abraham, and Ephraim Oratz. *The Psalms: Hebrew Text & English Translation with an Introduction and Commentary*. London: Soncino Press, 1992.

Cohen, Shaye J. D. *From the Maccabees to the Mishnah*. Louisville, KY: Westminster John Knox Press, 1987.

Cohen, Shaye J. D. *The Beginnings of Jewishness: Boundaries, Varieties, Uncertainties*. Berkeley: Univ. of California Press, 2009.

Cohen, Shaye J. D. "The Temple and the Synagogue." In *The Cambridge History of Judaism, Vol. 3: The Early Roman Period*. Cambridge: Cambridge University Press, 2008.

"Crete, Greece." *Jewish Virtual Library*. https://www.JewishVirtualLibrary.org/crete.

Davies, William David. *Paul and Rabbinic Judaism: Some Rabbinic Elements in Pauline Theology*. London: SPCK, 1970.

"Elder." *Jewish Virtual Library*. https://www.JewishVirtualLibrary.org/elder.

Finkelstein, Louis, W. D. Davies, and William Horbury. *The Cambridge History of Judaism*. Cambridge: Cambridge University Press, 1999.

Flusser, David. *Judaism and the Origins of Christianity*. Jerusalem: Magnes Press, Hebrew University, 1988.

Gaebelein, Frank E. *The Expositor's Bible Commentary: With the New International Version of the Holy Bible (Volume 9)*. Grand Rapids: Regency Reference Library, 1984.

Gaebelein, Frank E., et al. *The Expositor's Bible Commentary, Volume 11: Ephesians, Philippians, Colossians, Thessalonians 1 & 2, Timothy 1 & 2, Titus, Philemon*. Grand Rapids: Zondervan, 1978.

Grimm, Carl Ludwig Wilibald, et al. *The New Thayer's Greek-English Lexicon of the New Testament: Being Grimm's Wilke's Clavis Novi Testamenti*. Peabody, MA: Hendrickson, 1981.

Guthrie, Donald. *The Pastoral Epistles*. Grand Rapids: Eerdmans, 1994.

Hagner, Donald A. *The Jewish Reclamation of Jesus: An Analysis and Critique of Modern Jewish Study of Jesus*. Grand Rapids: Academie Books, 1986.

Hanson, Anthony Tyrrell. *The Pastoral Epistles: Based on the Revised Standard Version*. Grand Rapids: Eerdmans, 1987.

Hezser, Catherine. "Responses to Suffering in Classical Rabbinic Literature." *Hebrew Studies*. October 5, 1995. https://www.jstor.org/stable/i27909446.

Hirsch, Emil G. "Servant of God." *JewishEncyclopedia.com.* http://www.JewishEncyclopedia.com/articles/13444-servant-of-god.

Hirshman, Marc. "Origen's View of 'Jewish Fables' in Genesis." In Grypeou, Emmanouela, and Helen Spurling, eds., *The Exegetical Encounter Between Jews and Christians in Late Antiquity*. Leiden: Brill, 2009.

Hort, F. J. A. *Judaistic Christianity: A Course of Lectures*. n.p., 1894.

Humphreys, A. E. *The Epistles to Timothy and Titus*. Cambridge: University Press, 1901.

"Johanan ben Zakkai." *Jewish Virtual Library*. https://www.JewishVirtualLibrary.org/johanan-ben-zakkai.

Kirby, Peter. "e-Catena: Compiled Allusions to the NT in the Ante-Nicene Fathers – Titus." *Early Christian Writings*. www.EarlyChristianWritings.com/e-catena/titus1.html.

Krauss, Samuel. *The Jews in the Works of the Church Fathers: Sources for Understanding the Agaddah: 67 (Analecta Gorgiana)*. Piscataway, NJ: Gorgias Press, 2008.

Köstenberger, Andreas J. *Commentary on 1–2 Timothy & Titus*. Nashville: Holman Reference, 2017.

Lachs, Samuel Tobias. *A Rabbinic Commentary on the New Testament: The Gospels of Matthew, Mark, and Luke*. Hoboken, NJ: KTAV, 1987.

Le Cornu, Hilary, and Joseph Shulam. *A Commentary on the Jewish Roots of Acts*. Jerusalem: Netivyah Bible Instruction Ministry, 2003.

Levine, Amy-Jill, and Marc Zvi Brettler. *The Jewish Annotated New Testament: New Revised Standard Version Bible Translation*. New York: Oxford University Press, 2017.

Levine, Lee I. "The Nature and Origin of the Palestinian Synagogue Reconsidered." *Journal of Biblical Literature* Vol. 115, No. 3 (1996): 425. https://doi.org/10.2307/3266895.

Longenecker, Richard N. *The Christology of Early Jewish Christianity*. Vancouver, B.C.: Regent College Bookstore, 1994.

Marshall, I. Howard. "The Significance of Pentecost." *Scottish Journal of Theology* Vol. 30, No. 4 (1977): 347–69. https://doi.org/10.1017/s003693060002617x.

Miller, Chaim. *Chumash: The Five Books of Moses: With Rashi's Commentary, Targum Onkelos and Haftaros With a Commentary Anthologized From Classic Rabbinic Texts and the Works of the Lubavitcher Rebbe*. New York: Kol Menachem, 2006.

"Halakhah: The Laws of Jewish Life." *My Jewish Learning*. www.MyJewishLearning.com/article/halakhah-the-laws-of-jewish-life.

Neusner, Jacob. *Judaism in the Beginning of Christianity*. Philadelphia: Fortress Press, 1988.

Oden, Thomas C. *Pastoral Theology*. Grand Rapids: Zondervan, 2012.

Pietersma, Albert, and Benjamin Givens Wright. "The Twelve Prophets." In *A New English Translation of the Septuagint: and the Other Greek Translations Traditionally Included Under That Title*. New York: Oxford University Press, 2007.

Quinn, Jerome D. *The Anchor Bible: A New Translation with Notes and Commentary and an Introduction to Titus, I and II Timothy, the Pastoral Epistles*. New York: Doubleday, 1990.

Reif, Stefan C. *Judaism and Hebrew Prayer: New Perspectives on Jewish Liturgical History*. Cambridge: Cambridge University Press, 1998.

"Religion: Christianity." *Jewish Virtual Library*. www.JewishVirtualLibrary.org/christianity-2.

Safrai, Shmuel. *The Literature of the Sages, First Part: Oral Tora, Halakha, Mishna, Tosefta, Talmud, External Tractates*. Philadelphia: Fortress Press, 1987.

Sanders, E. P. *Jewish Law from Jesus to the Mishnah: Five Studies*. London: SCM Press, 1990.

Sandmel, Samuel. *A Jewish Understanding of the New Testament*. Woodstock, VT: Jewish Lights Publishing, 2008.

Scherman, Nosson, et al. *Tanach: The Torah, Prophets, Writings: The Twenty-Four Books of the Bible, Newly Translated and Annotated*. Brooklyn: Mesorah Publications, 1996.

Scherman, Nosson. *The Chumash: The Torah, Haftaros and Five Megillos With a Commentary Anthologized from the Rabbinic Writings*. Brooklyn: Mesorah Publications, 2001.

Schiffman, Lawrence H. *From Text to Tradition: A History of Second Temple and Rabbinic Judaism*. Hoboken, NJ: KTAV, 1991.

Schiffman, Lawrence H. "How Jewish Christians Became Christians." *My Jewish Learning*. https://www.MyJewishLearning.com/article/how-jewish-christians-became-christians.

Shulam, Joseph, and Hilary Le Cornu. *A Commentary on the Jewish Roots of Romans*. Baltimore: Messianic Jewish Publishers, 1998.

Spencer, Aída Besançon. *2 Timothy and Titus: A New Covenant Commentary*. Eugene, OR: Cascade Books, 2014.

Spicq, Ceslas. *Saint Paul: Les Épîtres Pastorales*. Paris: Lecoffre, 1969.

Steinsaltz, Rabbi Adin, and Israel V. Berman. *The Talmud: The Steinsaltz Edition*. New York: Random House, 1990.

Steinsaltz, Rabbi Adin. "Berakhot 62a." *Sefaria. Koren Noé Talmud, William Davidson Digital Edition*. https://www.Sefaria.org/berakhot.

Stern, David H. *Jewish New Testament Commentary: A Companion Volume to the Jewish New Testament*. Clarksville, MD: Jewish New Testament Publications, 1999.

Stern, David H. *Jewish New Testament: A Translation of the New Testament That Expresses Its Jewishness*. Clarksville, MD: Jewish New Testament Publications, 1998.

Tashjian, Jirair. "Life in Crete at the Time of Titus." *Sunday Teacher*. https://SundayTeacher.com/vcmedia/2414/2414925.pdf.

Theron, Daniel J. *Evidence of Tradition; Selected Source Material for the Study of the History of the Early Church, Introduction and Canon of the New Testament*. London: Bowes & Bowes, 1957.

Vogelstein, Hermann. *The Development of the Apostolate in Judaism and Its Transformation in Christianity*. Cincinnati: Union of American Hebrew Congregations, 1925.

Zahavy, Tzvee. "It Is Not in Heaven: Judaic Systems, Laws and Discordant Discourses." https://www.tzvee.com/Home/it-is-not-in-heaven.

Zeitlin, Irving M. *Jesus and the Judaism of His Time*. Cambridge: Polity Press, 1994.

Zondervan NIV Study Bible. Grand Rapids: Zondervan, 2008.

Messianic Jewish
Publishers & Resources

We are a three-fold ministry, reaching Jewish people with the message of Messiah, teaching our non-Jewish spiritual family about their Jewish roots, and strengthening congregations with excellent resources.

Over 100 Messianic Jewish Books, Bibles & Commentaries available at your favorite Bookstore.

Endorsed by Christian Leaders and Theologians:

Dr. Jack Hayford
Dr. Walter C. Kaiser, Jr.
Dr. Marvin Wilson
Ken Taylor
Stephen Strang
Dr. R.C. Sproul
Coach Bill McCartney
and more!

800-410-7367
www.MessianicJewish.net

Printed in the United States
by Baker & Taylor Publisher Services